100 Ideas for Primary Teachers:

Engaging Parents

Other titles in the 100 Ideas for Primary Teachers series:

100 Ideas for Primary Teachers:

Engaging Parents

Janet Goodall and Kathryn Weston

BLOOMSBURY EDUCATION

LONDON   OXFORD   NEW YORK   NEW DELHI   SYDNEY

BLOOMSBURY EDUCATION
Bloomsbury Publishing Plc
50 Bedford Square, London, WC1B 3DP, UK

BLOOMSBURY, BLOOMSBURY EDUCATION and
the Diana logo are trademarks of Bloomsbury Publishing Plc

First published in Great Britain, 2018 by Bloomsbury Publishing Plc

A catalogue record for this book is available from the British Library

ISBN: PB: 978-1-4729-5520-3; ePDF: 978-1-4729-5519-7;
ePub: 978-1-4729-5518-0

4 6 8 10 9 7 5 3

Typeset by Newgen KnowledgeWorks Pvt. Ltd., Chennai, India
Printed and bound in the UK by CPI Group (UK) Ltd., Croydon CR0 4YY

To find out more about our authors and books visit
www.bloomsbury.com and sign up for our newsletters.

Contents

Acknowledgements

I would like to express my thanks to the many school staff and parents who have worked with me through the years, and to my family who have supported me through the period of working on this book. (Dr Janet Goodall)

I would like to thank Sally Graham (1954–2017), a great educator and beloved colleague, who first inspired my interest in working with parents. (Dr Kathryn Weston)

Both authors owe particular thanks to Catherine Goodall (who advised us on the section dealing with children in the care system), and to Hannah Marston from Bloomsbury, who has been hugely supportive during the writing process.

Introduction

Engaging parents is one of the things that schools think is a great idea in principle, but many struggle to think of ways to do so effectively. As we make clear in this book, there is a big difference between inviting parents along to cake sales, for example, and engaging with them in a manner that will truly boost children's learning outcomes. The question of *why* schools should engage with parents is easily answered by considering the research evidence. There is an unequivocal relationship between parental self-efficacy and a child's ability to thrive. By taking steps to engage parents in a child's journey through school, teachers are reaching out as partners and ensuring that the bridge between home and school remains a sturdy one. Children can thrive when schools and families work together, in partnership, with their values and ethos aligned as far as possible.

Working with parents and families shouldn't be an arduous task – rather, a rewarding one. By adopting our tips, you will be well on your way to meaningful parental engagement. We don't expect you to adopt *every* tip; our hope is that a few will resonate with you and colleagues, and you will feel able to confidently 'try and apply' those. Whichever you select, constantly evaluating how parents respond to any new idea or change in working practice will be an integral part of judging success.

Our tips aren't just about everyday teaching practice. We are lobbying for a wider change too, concerning the fundamental ethos of schools. Today, teachers are expected to be all things to all people. You need to be able to return to the job that you are trained to do and really focus on learning. In challenging times, parents and families are a school's greatest resource for support, encouragement and assistance when it comes to helping children progress.

You might think it will be hard to get colleagues and parents on board with a new way of thinking in your school, but be patient; this is an iterative process. As you change your practices and beliefs, those of colleagues will change and evolve too. It's far better to do one or two small things, and to make incremental changes, than to do nothing at all! Eventually, we hope that your school will be able to adopt a holistic approach to engaging parents that all staff understand the value of and are committed to.

We encourage you to:

- Share the ideas in this book with colleagues, if you can – not only are two heads better than one, but many hands make light work!
- Adapt or tweak things that we suggest. After all, that's what good teachers do!

Engaging with parents more effectively can improve almost all aspects of school life, make things run more smoothly, save you time in the long run, and support pupil achievement. *Why would you not want to read this book?*

The first part of the book will help you into the right frame of mind to engage with parents. It focuses on the 'why' and underlines the differences between *involving* as opposed to *engaging* with them. We encourage you to anticipate any barriers to engaging parents in your particular setting and to carefully consider what true partnership looks and feels like.

Understanding your parents is the first step in supporting them. In Parts 2 and 3, we suggest lots of background ideas and activities that will help you understand your families better, and support them as effectively as possible. Every family is different and every parent is different, just like every child in your class is different. But you still find ways to teach all of your pupils, and you will find ways to support all of your families too. Remember what you have in common: you both want the best for the children.

The final four parts of the book are about setting up and planning holistic parental engagement strategies. After all, parental engagement with children's learning doesn't just happen – it needs some consideration. We give lots of ideas about the behind-the-scenes work that will facilitate support for parental engagement across your school.

Enjoy our tips, while remembering to pull out what's best and what's feasible for you, your school and the families you work with.

How to use this book

This book includes quick, easy and practical ideas for you to dip in and out of, to support you in planning and conducting effective parental engagement.

Each section has:

- a catchy title, easy to refer to and share with your colleagues
- an interesting quote linked to the idea
- a summary of the idea in bold, making it easy to flick through the book and identify an idea you want to use at a glance
- a step-by-step guide to implementing the idea.

Each idea also includes one or more of the following:

Teaching tip

Practical tips and advice for how and how not to run the activity or put the idea into practice.

Taking it further

Ideas and advice for how to extend the idea or develop it further.

Bonus idea ★

There are 36 bonus ideas in this book that are extra exciting, extra original and extra interesting.

Share how you use these ideas and find out what other practitioners have done using **#100ideas**.

Online resources also accompany this book. When a resource is referenced in the book, follow the link www.bloomsbury.com/100-ideas-primary-engaging-parents to find extra resources, catalogued under the relevant idea number. Here you can also find the full list of website addresses mentioned in the book.

Background

Part 1

Why bother engaging parents?

'When you see parents as true partners in pupils' learning, children begin to thrive. Parental engagement is the golden key that can unlock the door to pupils reaching their potential.'

Parental engagement in learning is an important part of children's learning process.

We have an achievement gap between children from different socio-economic backgrounds. This gap is apparent by the time children start school, and doesn't get much better once they are there.

We also know that up to 80 per cent of the gap is attributable to things that happen *outside of school*. Supporting parents to support children's learning is the best available approach to help narrow that gap.

Most parents want to support their children's learning, but for lots of reasons, some don't feel able, or confident, to do so. Many parents also don't realise how important their support can be – or how to ask for help to support learning.

Working in partnership with parents means that children experience support for learning that doesn't end when they leave the school gate. Parental engagement in learning can help:

- improve behaviour in school
- increase rates of homework return
- improve children's academic outcomes.

Going beyond involvement

'Getting parents to attend functions, cake sales, fairs and fêtes equates to parental involvement, but it is when the school enables parents to confidently support their children's learning at home that the magic happens!'

Parental engagement in children's learning is about a lot more than 'getting parents in'.

It is important to say at the outset that, although this book presents a series of tips and ideas, what we're advocating here is much more than a surface-level, cosmetic add-on to school life. Putting parental engagement with children's learning into place requires a fundamental change of belief around what we're doing in schools. Part of that change in belief will come through working through the tips presented here: it is an iterative process.

Parental engagement in children's learning can be defined as parents' engagement in the broad sphere of their children's learning – that means it's not defined by parents coming into school.

We need to go beyond thinking about how parents interact with *the school* and start thinking about, and supporting, how they interact with *learning*, and how we can support them to do that in partnership with the school. Parental engagement with children's learning is about helping parents support learning outside of school. It is *not* just about helping with homework; it *is* about all learning, all the time.

Teaching tip

It is important for teachers to understand that parental engagement with children's learning takes place mainly away from school – at home, in the car – through everyday family activities.

The home learning environment

'Eighty per cent of the factors affecting how well children do at school are dependent on what happens outside the school gates – whether it is in the home or in the wider community.'

Research shows that it's what parents do with their children, not what level of education they have or how much money they have, that makes a difference to children's learning.

Teaching tip

Creating a home learning environment shouldn't feel onerous for families. Reassure parents that it's the simple things that can make the biggest difference!

By 'home learning environment' we mean all the learning that happens outside of school – everything from learning to walk and talk to learning to share, even table manners. But this includes the support that families give to schooling as well – from helping with homework to discussions about learning, reading and sharing stories together, even to asking, 'How was your day?' (see Idea 71).

The attitude towards learning in the home is vital for children's achievement. We need to support parents to keep that attitude positive and creative, so that at 15, young people are still as keen to ask the 'why' questions as they are at five. Some of the following will help ensure the home learning environment is as rich and supportive as the school environment.

- Let parents know that it's important they tell their children that they as parents value education and school. Parents set the tone at home with expectations about learning.
- Let parents know that they are already experts on their child and that you are picking up the baton when their child enters your classroom and building on the work that they have already done nurturing that child; both groups (school and home) need to work together.

- Give parents tips on how to support learning (there are lots of these in this book!).
- Let parents know it's ok to say 'I don't know – let's find out!'. Share with them how you encourage children to find out the answer in the classroom. What pointers can you give parents?
- Help parents understand the importance of play, songs, nursery rhymes and outdoor activity for learning. Without an understanding of the importance of these activities for children's cognitive, social and emotional development, some parents may not do them.
- When parents understand that they have a powerful role to play in shaping a child's educational outcomes, they are often more willing to engage with their children's learning.

Taking it further

Talk to other teachers in other schools – learn from what others are doing!

Saving time, money and school resources

'Once parents understood how they could help their children with the project, they offered great suggestions and ideas that fed into my teaching. With parents on board, my job is so much easier.'

We know how busy teachers are, but when a school engages holistically with parents around learning, it can truly save everyone time in the long run.

One of the things we advocate in this book is the need to do things that work and to stop doing things that don't work. By this we mean it is important for schools to evaluate how effective a given parental engagement strategy is, and if it is not working, to try something else instead. Being flexible, open-minded and innovative really helps when it comes to finding ways of working successfully with parents and families. Here is how this book can help:

- The parental census (Idea 23) will help you find out what's important to your families.
- Setting a vision (Idea 32) will help you decide what your aim is in engaging parents.
- The wish list (Idea 30) will help you decide what it is you want to do to achieve that aim.
- The evaluation idea (Idea 36) will help you appreciate what is, and is not, working.
- The online resources for this book will offer ready-made and adaptable materials to support you.

In developing a clear plan of action that stems from consultation with parents and staff and is subject to continual evaluation, you will save time in the long run.

Working in partnership

'Parents know I'm on their side. We both want what's best for their children.'

Partnership with parents is both a goal to be achieved and a way of working.

Most of us have been involved in projects that didn't work well because not everyone involved was singing from the same hymn sheet, as it were. Children's learning is no different: it will be much better supported if all those around the child work together, towards the same ends.

And, importantly, it will all work better if everyone involved in the process does this explicitly, with appropriate knowledge of what, to continue the metaphor, the other singers are doing and what notes everyone is expected to be singing at any given point.

Equality is vital in partnerships. But this doesn't mean everyone has the same jobs, skills or talents. It does mean, though, that everyone respects the other members of the partnership. Respect for parents, and the part they can play in children's learning, is a fundamental building block of this partnership.

> **Taking it further**
>
> Try to define what 'partnership' means to you, in the abstract, then see how that definition can be applied to working with parents.

Keep the focus on learning

'Getting your priorities right underpins everything else – and learning has to be the number one priority.'

Everything schools, and school staff, do is secondary to learning and needs to be judged against learning as a standard.

Schools exist for one reason: to support the societally-agreed learning of young people – and within learning, we include a wide variety of things, such as 'learning to be well' in all senses of the word. This emphasis on learning is also vital in relation to engaging parents in children's learning – so that children will have the best chances in life.

Here are some strategies to help you maintain learning at the centre of all you do:

- Keep asking yourself, and your colleagues, 'What does this have to do with learning?'.
- Consider whether or not things really need to be done, if their connection to learning is tenuous or difficult to find.
- Suggest that 'What does this have to do with learning?' becomes a part of every meeting or discussion.
- Look at all new initiatives through the lens of learning: how will this make learning better? Or, how can I use this to make learning better in my classroom?

Keep learning at the forefront of connections with parents: that's what this is all about. Make a list of all the information you send home in a given term. Out of this, make a (usually much smaller) list of the things that *actually relate to learning*. Do you really need to be sending the rest of this home?

Don't panic – you already have the skills you need

'Even though working with parents probably didn't feature in your initial teacher training, you already have a lot of the skills you will need to do it effectively.'

You are already a highly-skilled professional – and becoming more highly skilled with each passing year. Those skills don't only relate to working with children, but to working with their parents, too.

We are not suggesting that you treat parents like pupils. We are, however, encouraging you to reflect on the array of existing skills that you already have around supporting learning; we suggest that these can serve you well when working with parents. Here are our recommendations:

Teaching tip

See the online resources for this book for an event-planning template.

- When you plan an event for parents, treat it as you would a lesson plan. What are the objectives? What do you want parents to take away from the event? And how will you know whether or not that has happened?
- Make a list of the things that you want to do around supporting parental engagement.
- On that list, make a note of the skills, materials and other things that will be needed.
- Be honest about your own skills – but don't play down what you can already do.
- Treat every encounter with parents as a learning opportunity, just as you do every encounter with your pupils.
- Include interactions with parents in your reflections on your teaching.

Don't judge – perceptions are important

'I thought one mum didn't come to parents' evening because she wasn't interested in her child's progress. Turned out she was wary of teachers because of her own difficult childhood and school experience.'

It's very easy to be judgemental about how other people raise their children, but most of us have been on the receiving end of that sort of judgement and know how hurtful it can be.

Have you ever had someone judge you harshly when they only understood part of the situation? Most of us have been there, and most of us have found it an uncomfortable place to be.

If you're a parent, you know this all too well. And if you're working in a school, it's sometimes very hard to *avoid* making those judgements. But there are a few things to note:

- Research shows that school staff often underestimate what parents are *already* doing at home to support learning.
- Remember that coming into school is not the most important part of parental engagement with learning; the main site of engagement is at home.
- Think about how your words and actions are perceived. Parents have often reported that they feel that staff are looking down on them. That may well not be the case – but perceptions are powerful.
- Consider how it would feel to be on the receiving end of the phone call or letter you're about to send home before you do it.
- Remember, just like children and colleagues, parents need encouragement and praise.

Anticipate barriers

'Some barriers to engagement – stress, employment, working more than one job, wide-ranging family commitments – you can't address. But other things may be considerably easier to deal with.'

Brainstorm with colleagues about possible barriers to effective parent partnership and how to work to overcome them.

Try making a list of possible reasons for lack of engagement. Examples might include a lack of interest; lack of transport; childcare/other caring issues; English as an additional language. Now, instead of treating these as problems inherent in parents, try to see them as barriers to overcome or to help parents overcome.

This is a two-step process: the temptation is to jump immediately into finding or suggesting solutions but, particularly for some issues, this misses an important step of understanding either why the barrier exists in the first place or how it affects parents' engagement. For example, do you really *know* that parents aren't interested in their children's learning? Are they unwilling or simply unable to come to school (which is certainly not the same thing)?

Here are some suggestions for tackling common barriers:

- Ensure that you have easy access to the transport information that your parents need. When does the last bus leave school that will get parents home in the evening? Use these timetables to plan events.
- Have a crèche available for times you expect parents to be in school for more than a few minutes.
- Be mindful of other commitments that communities and families may have. If a World Cup football game is on the same day, you will have lots of empty seats!

Teaching tip

Consider having a 'solutions board' in the staffroom where colleagues can chip in with ideas for increasing parent partnership and engagement.

Bonus idea ★

Sometimes a local nursery nearby is happy to send along a few members of staff to create a pop-up crèche for the evening. They get to advertise themselves to parents, and you get the opportunity to work with parents who aren't distracted by younger children.

Think beyond the classroom

'Children spend more time out of school than in – but that doesn't mean they're not learning!'

Your school can become a hub for community activity, working to bring people together. This idea offers some simple ways of achieving this.

Your school should be used as far as possible by the local community. Think of ways of opening up the school to local networks.

Parents have a great appetite for attending talks by interesting people where there is no requirement on them to participate other than through listening. There is no reason why your school can't become a hub of activity for such a speaker series.

Your school may not even need to bring in external speakers as there are always brilliant story-tellers within every parenting community. If you are stuck on what parents might be interested in hearing about, refer to the parent census (see Idea 23). What stories might parents have that others might want to hear?

Remember, families and the community around the school are rich resources that are traditionally under-used when it comes to learning. Every parent and every family will have their own network to tap into. When parents do contribute to school life in this way, it demonstrates true partnership. Consider inviting parents in to talk about their jobs/work/volunteering, both to children during the day and to career evenings for families.

Bonus idea ★

One school has a mums' group that comes in and uses the sewing machines in school. Even if you don't have a bank of sewing machines, what other resources could you share with parents?

Raising aspirations

'As a school, we are ambitious for all our children, not just those who would traditionally be expected to do well.'

Research has shown that most parents have high aspirations for their young children and that these aspirations need support to stay high as children grow.

It is important that both parents and schools set high but *realistic* aspirations for children. There are lots of ways that schools can promote an 'aiming high' culture. Often, it is less about posters displayed in corridors and more about modelling goal-setting, sharing achievements and teaching children how to overcome an 'I can't' attitude.

- See if there are programmes/organisations that will support your school to encourage high ambitions and aspirations.
- Create opportunities for children to meet a variety of people in different job roles while they are at primary school. These can come from the parenting community, nearby universities or colleges, or from the wider community. Try to challenge gender stereotypical assumptions. One primary school that we worked with invited in a decorated (female) naval commander of a warship to address an audience of young boys. She certainly made an impression!
- Ask staff to share the dreams and ambitions they had when they were growing up.
- Consider making blue plaques, like the ones found on buildings, for successful alumni from the school.

Teaching tip

Attracting alumni to any school is a fun way of showing pupils that there is a world beyond school and depending on the career pathway of the alumni, their stories will inspire parents and children.

Taking it further

Every member of staff could visibly display a goal they are working towards on their classroom door. These could be related to learning (doing an MA for example) or something entirely different, such as attending obedience classes with a new puppy. Make aiming high visible!

School readiness

'School readiness isn't solely the responsibility of schools – parents, families and schools all have a part to play.'

School readiness is a measure of how prepared a child is to succeed in school cognitively, socially and emotionally, but it also relates to how ready the school is to receive the child.

Teaching tip

A mobile-friendly website is an ideal place for any parent-facing information.

We often talk about children being 'school ready' in developmental terms but taking that phrase apart can uncover some interesting assumptions. We know that children from lower socio-economic backgrounds often start school months, and sometimes even almost a year behind their more advantaged peers. They are often not, in the view of schools, 'ready'; they don't have the language, the motor and social skills that school staff expect.

But school readiness isn't just about the child and family – it's also about *the school* being ready for the children who will arrive.

At first hearing, this sounds rather odd – how can *schools* not be school ready? It's better to rephrase this: schools need to be ready for the children who arrive, for *all* the children, rather than just the few who might fit into expectations. This requires more on the part of school staff than waiting passively to assess the new arrivals. Be proactive by:

- Trying to find out as much as you can about the children in advance – from pre-schools, childminders, Early Years centres, etc.
- Including information about skills children will ideally have at the start of school (e.g. should they be able to put on their own coats?) when preparing information for parents.
- Considering creating a transition package for families to read ahead of arrival.

- Adding a section to the school website called 'Getting ready for school', packed with little film clips showing parents around the school. Be friendly and welcoming, explaining how parents can give their children a head-start by doing certain activities with them ahead of the new term.
- Considering the inclusion of a bank of songs and nursery rhymes on your website for parents to tap into.
- With each passing cohort, consciously building a clear picture of what children generally do and do not know as they come in. Use this information to inform the support you're preparing for parents, as well as to inform your own practice and expectations.
- Asking current parents what they wish they had known or what would have helped them. Can they help prepare your materials for new parents?
- Creating a parent buddy system where current parents can support new ones.

Taking it further

Remember you can involve pupils or existing parents in any video clips. Hearing from existing parents can really put new parents at ease.

Beware the power-play

'Schools can be scary, intimidating places for people who don't work in them – particularly parents.'

Noticing and dealing with power relationships is an important part of improving your work with parents.

It's odd, but true, that in many parent/teacher encounters, both parties feel that the other has the power. So how can we get over that?

- Watch out for how people are addressed. If you are Mrs or Mr Smith, don't call parents by their first names or refer to them as 'someone's dad'. Keep things on an equal footing – if you are Mr/Mrs/Ms, then parents should get an honorific too.
- Remember that parents approaching you with a problem are likely to be very worried not only about their child, but about how they will be received by staff – will staff look down on them for 'not being able to cope' or fob off their worries?
- Consider things like classroom layouts for meetings – is it really necessary to sit across from parents at parents' evening? Could you sit next to them, so you can both look at books and work together?
- Always watch the body language between you and a parent in any given situation. Try to ensure you remain as open and friendly as possible.

Ofsted/Estyn expectations

'We want a holistic approach to parental engagement that takes a whole-school approach to working with families.'

Inspectors want to know how you are working with parents. All the tips in this book will help you get on the right track, but we suggest you don't wait until you get the call from Ofsted, or in Wales Estyn, to take action!

In terms of school leadership and governance, inspection bodies certainly value parental contribution; parents' views are considered before and during inspections. School leaders are expected to share their vision for how parents and school can work together and to demonstrate efforts that the school has made to better support parents when it comes to pupils' learning.

In judging the *quality of teaching, learning and assessment,* inspectors will evaluate the extent to which schools communicate with parents and families in a timely and clear way.

- See the ideas on communication in Part 5 to help you do this effectively.
- Use record-keeping (Idea 35) to be able to prove that you do it.
- Ensure that your governors are on board with what you are doing about engaging parents because they will have to answer to inspectors about it.
- Use the suggestions in Idea 61 so that parents are aware of all you're doing as well!

Consider going beyond the simple need to *tell* parents – and move to the higher level of *working in partnership with parents*.

Understanding parents

Part 2

The first – and continuing – teachers of children

'Parents are a child's first teacher. What goes on at home can fundamentally shape a child's views of the world and approaches to learning and life.'

Working in partnership with parents starts with realising how important they are to children's learning.

When you think of how much a child has learned by the time he or she gets to school, the phrase 'parents are the first teachers' makes sense – children learn to walk, talk, share, and interact with others long before they get to school (even if they can't tie their shoelaces!).

Parents' support for learning does not stop on the first day of school, however. The research evidence is consistent: parents' continued interest in, and support for, their child's learning has a clear and definite effect on children's attendance, behaviour and attainment.

Here are the key points to remember as you work to develop a close partnership with parents:

- 'Learning' is much wider than 'schooling' and working in partnership with each other is in the best interest of the child.
- Parents need to know how important their continued support for learning is.
- Parents need to know *how* to support learning at home (and we have lots of suggestions about how to promote this in Part 6!).
- Recognising parents as being involved in their children's learning underpins all the rest of your work in this area.

Supporting family learning

'Now we look at everything as an opportunity to engage parents in children's learning.' (School governor)

Children don't exist in isolation. Most of the children in your class are immersed in a family of some sort.

Although we've talked a good deal about 'parents' and 'parental engagement with children's learning', we might just as easily (and perhaps more accurately) have talked about 'family engagement'.

Families, of course, come in all different shapes and sizes – and it's important not only to remember that, but to be seen to affirm it as well. Many of the sections in this book have ideas about including other family members in children's learning. This isn't a bonus or an add-on extra; it is a fundamental part of a child's learning process. Here are some underlying principles that we believe should underpin the school-family partnership.

- Approach every learning opportunity, especially homework, with an eye to how to involve the wider family (see Idea 67).
- Check resources available to staff, children and parents – do they portray a given family type as the norm, even just by being seen more often?
- If you know your families, you are in a better position to ensure that resources, posters around the school and sent-home information reflect the make-up of your school population.
- Invite parents in to talk about their experiences of learning, through the lens of different cultures and backgrounds.
- See also Idea 34 about how to embed parental engagement in school policies.

Teaching tip

See Idea 19 for how best to support children who have experience of the care system.

Taking it further

Consider a project at the start of the school year that encourages children to think about and articulate the different types of family units that exist within the school community. This will set the tone for an inclusive approach to family learning. Carers who are not mum and dad will feel more at ease knowing that the school considers them just as important!

'Parent' is a catch-all term – be careful how you use it

'I am his step-grandad and main carer. I was worried the school wouldn't see me as the most important person in his life, but I am.'

Lots of people who aren't technically parents (noun, plural), parent (verb)!

Teaching tip

Avoid giving the impression that fathers and grandfathers who are looking after their children are 'babysitting' rather than 'parenting'.

When we use the term 'parent', we mean 'any adult with a caring responsibility for the child'. In many cases, this will be one or both actual parents of the child. However, for more than 200,000 children in England, the person who looks after them is not a parent, but could be a grandparent, aunt or uncle, other relative or foster carer. When thinking about engaging 'parents' in children's learning, remember that not all of the adults involved will be parents.

- Avoid using phrases like 'Make sure Mummy sees this'; rather, use phrases that don't show an expectation that there will be a mum in the picture or that she has primary responsibility. Try saying, 'Make sure this gets signed', or 'Make sure this gets seen at home'.
- When you're looking for parent governors, are you open to the idea of the post being taken by a grandparent or carer? Make sure families know who can stand for these roles.
- Do you know who has the primary responsibility for caring for a child at any given time? This will be somewhere in the child's records, but are the records updated regularly? A parental support worker or teaching assistant may keep these records up to date as part of their role.

Bonus idea ★

In some communities, one grandparent may have many family members in school – consider how you could use that to your advantage to engage the family!

Dad, Grandad, Auntie and Uncle Tom Cobley and all

'I think schools need to do more to normalise dads volunteering and working with the school. Sometimes you feel like a fish out of water and everyone is wondering why you aren't at work!'

Be careful not to make assumptions about people who care for children. Not all primary carers are women.

We make a number of assumptions that feed into this understanding of 'parent = mum': that all children have a mum; that all mums are involved in learning; that they have a good deal of free time; and that even if a child does have a mum and a dad at home, it's mum who will be involved in school and schooling.

A lot of these assumptions just don't hold water for many children. Not all children have a mum at home and many may be cared for as much by grandparents as by parents. Nor should we think that interacting with school or learning is mum's job rather than dad's; more and more fathers want to be involved in their children's lives. And assuming that mums have the time and energy to be involved may just be another way of exploiting women's unpaid labour.

- Have a look at the displays around school. Will grandparents see displays that show older people, or do all the posters show young parents, particularly mums?
- Some men might feel more comfortable coming into school to an event specifically for males – how about something around Father's Day? (But make sure all male carers are welcome – not just dads!)
- If there's an opportunity to bring male carers into the school to talk about the work that they do or hobbies that they have, take it!

Teaching tip

One of the schools we've been working with opened their breakfast club to parents, calling it 'Bacon Butties and Books'. Aimed particularly at dads/male carers, the idea was to give men a chance to share a meal and a book with their children. It was very successful!

Not every child is in a family

'We had only been fostering him for three weeks when I had to attend parents' evening. The teacher started the conversation saying what a great job I was doing and it felt amazing!'

Children with experience of being in care still need adults to support their learning – perhaps even more so.

While this book talks about supporting parents' engagement with learning, we have already made the point that 'parent' can be a very broad term – and it needs to be broad enough to include support for children who are living in foster or other care. Over 70,000 children in the UK were in the care system in 2016, out of 8.2 million in school overall.

We know it can be difficult and confusing to deal with the bureaucracy that accompanies children in care, and to figure out who is the best person to contact for specific issues. In some ways, that means it's *more* important to ensure that children in care get all the support they can, including support from adults outside of school.

- Make sure school records are up to date for all children, including those in the care system.
- We know that social workers, police, etc. all use different forms, work to different schedules and have different criteria for success around children in the care system. We suggest that you concentrate on the child's *learning* and wellbeing in school – and work with others who are responsible for wider issues.
- Don't neglect to praise children in the care system to relevant adults and let the child know that you are passing on good news about them.

Parents as partners (not problems!)

'Working in partnership with parents is the best way to support children's learning and achievement.'

If we are to support our children's achievement we need to move beyond the model of parents as 'teacher's helper'. That model immediately establishes a relationship which puts schools firmly in the driving seat, with parents – at best – just passengers.

We've seen that one of the main foundations of children's achievement is the attitude towards learning in the home – what we call the home learning environment. What parents *do* is far more important than who parents are, or what qualifications they have. Try to follow these guidelines:

Teaching tip

Remember to share with colleagues your own positive experiences of working with parents and families.

- Avoid seeing parents as 'problems' that need to be managed, or as people not really able to offer effective support.
- Think of children holistically – as members of families and wider communities, not just as 'pupils' in your class. This can help you to see the part that parents can contribute to their learning.
- Reassure parents that the most important thing they can do to support learning is to show an interest – they do not need to know the answers.
- Think about parents as full partners in supporting children's learning. This doesn't mean that they do the same job as school staff – partners aren't identical and often have quite different jobs.
- Remember what brings you together with parents in the first place – doing the best for their child!

Not all parents are the same

'When schools take the time to get to know their parents and families during transition, this is not time wasted. It enables the school to really hit the ground running at the start of term.'

Just as we differentiate among children because they are not all the same, so we need to view each family as a unique case: parents (widely defined) aren't all the same!

If you're asked to take over a new class, you're very likely to say something like, 'Tell me what I need to know'. You're asking which child needs a bit more support, who needs a challenge, who might need a bit more attention. You do this because you know that no two children are the same, no two learn in precisely the same way and no two classes are the same. Differentiating between pupils' individual differences is a familiar part of being a teacher. Yet we all too often forget or neglect this skill when it comes to dealing with parents.

- Before putting in place initiatives to support different parents and families, do a basic audit of the parenting community. Ask your parents what support they think is required to help them engage with their children's learning (see Idea 23).
- By exploring parental views and expectations, you may come across cultural factors that influence the degree to which parents expect to be involved in their child's learning. Don't be afraid to talk to parents about potential different experiences of education and schooling – in the end, schools can set the tone for a new approach that values and expects parental engagement.
- Don't underestimate the personal touch. One teacher told us, 'I phoned the pupil's mum and said, "I'm really worried about Sophie. What can you tell me that will help

me to help her?"' The teacher said that this made a big difference in the relationship with that parent. We can see why – it changed the power balance from 'teacher knows everything' to 'we're all in this together, for the pupil's benefit'.

- Be careful not to make assumptions about parents. The vast majority of parents love their children and want them to do well, but that doesn't mean that all parents know how best to support their children in the school system, or what will help children learn to read, for example. Equally, even if a parent holds a PhD in literature, it doesn't mean they know the best ways to support their child with their geography homework!

- Just as not all children are the same, not all children in the same family are the same! Don't assume that just because you've taught a child in a family before that you don't need to do the groundwork with that family.

Taking it further

Talk to a local community leader about how you (the school and that part of the community) can work together to support parents' engagement in learning.

Know your parents – a critical first step

'When I learned that two of my new pupils were recent refugees, I added some new books to my classroom library to help pupils understand why children might need to move countries and how it might feel.'

Just as it's much easier to teach children when you know about them, it's much easier to support parents when you know more about their lives.

Here are some ideas to help you find out more about the families and communities you work with:

- At the end of the summer term, send out a survey to the next cohort of arrivals into the school to capture as much information as possible about the children, their backgrounds, families, individual interests and hobbies. You can use a simple tool like Survey Monkey.
- Send out letters to the families telling them that the school is greatly looking forward to working with the whole family in partnership. You may want to include a link to resources that parents can dip into over the summer, available via your website. This may link to tips relating to school-readiness, for example (see Idea 12).
- Create a video talking about parent partnership – try to express an inclusive approach that celebrates all different types of families at the school. Include chats with existing and former parents of children at the school so that they can reflect on why their children enjoy school and their thoughts on how the school works with parents.
- Make it clear from the beginning that you are a school open to ideas and that you welcome the involvement of parents and families.

Home learning census

'The only way to work in partnership with someone is to understand what they're doing, and for them to understand what you're doing.'

One of the things that research has shown quite clearly is that school staff often underestimate what parents *already* do with their children, particularly in terms of supporting the home learning environment – things like environmental print and discussions about learning.

One way of both adding to your store of knowledge about families and showing families that you value what they are doing is simply to ask them (while being careful not to set up guilt-making expectations for parents).

Teaching tip

A template for this parents' census is available in the online resources for this book.

Here are some tips on how to get started when creating a survey or census to find out more about home learning:

- Don't ask parents to sign the forms or give their names – you're looking for a general overview. This will also prevent parents from feeling as though they are being judged.
- Remember, whether using the template for this census or creating your own, that the important bits of parental engagement are about the learning in the home – not just, or mainly, about helping with homework.
- Ask parents what they are already doing to support learning; if possible, and if it's appropriate for your parents, this can be a 'free text' answer – just a box they can fill in.
- If you use a drop-down list, still have an 'other' section people can fill in – and make your list as wide and inclusive as possible. Ask some of your parents for ideas!
- Remember to share the results of your survey with parents (see Idea 64), and celebrate what they are already doing.

Ask parents what they think

'Partnership goes both ways!'

Many parents are more than able to 'work the system' and let you know what they think is best for their child. Other parents might not have the confidence to do so. It's important to ensure that all voices are heard.

Some parents will have dreams, goals, aspirations and expectations around what the school can do for their child and where teachers will take them on their educational journey.

Many other parents are not able to articulate such aspirational goals; perhaps they lack the confidence to do so or they are simply unaware of the need to do so. Some may not even know that there are things that they could do at home that would support their child's learning or they may face other barriers, including lack of fluent English. Here are some ideas to help:

- Provide ample opportunities for parents to let you know what they want for their children and their ideas for how to make that happen. This could be through suggestion boxes in the playground or reception area of the school; it could be a section on the website or a dedicated email address or text account.
- Make sure that parents are able to make suggestions in their own language. Any comments can easily be translated later.
- Ensure that you let parents know what you are doing as a result of their ideas. If you can't follow up on their ideas, let them know why.
- When you have an opportunity to chat informally with parents, ask them what they think, e.g. Did you feel that parents' evening went well last night? Parents have lots of views and when they are heard, like anyone else, they feel valued.

Emphasise what you have in common

'I didn't realise how much the staff here care about my daughter – I feel so much happier leaving her here now!'

It's always easier to relate to people and to work well with them when you have something in common with them. This is true of parents and teachers – but sometimes, we need to make that common ground quite clear.

For years, we've been asking school staff why they got into teaching and why they stay, and the answer always comes down to some variant of, 'I want to make things better for young people'. For teachers, those aspirations for pupils are obvious – but your drive and commitment may not be obvious to parents.

- Part of making this clear to parents is letting them know that you actually have taken time to get to know their child. This can be through a simple comment such as, 'He always has a smile' or, 'How's the family dog?'
- Equally, although teachers are time-strapped, try to remember to give parents compliments about their child. A simple acknowledgement that they are doing a great job can go a very long way, e.g. 'Your daughter is so polite, she's a credit to you!'.
- Remember that parents know their children in a way that is different from the way you know them. They are experts in their own children's lives at home – that's expertise that is vital for children's learning!
- Ask parents to write a short note to the school before their child arrives: 'What it will help you to know about my child'. This could include things like, 'Samia loves dinosaurs' or 'John sometimes needs alone time'.

Taking it further

Ask a current parent what they would have written about their child before they started school. If you have your own children, write one for them as an example.

Banning 'hard to reach'

'I make sure my kids are clean and ready for school each day. But don't ask me to go to any school events. I don't really like school buildings — it brings back horrible memories of being told off.'

We are not suggesting that you ban parents who are thought to be hard to reach — rather, we want you to ban the label 'hard to reach' as applied to parents.

Teaching tip

Idea 9 is all about anticipating barriers.

Schools are full of labels. But not all labels are useful and some are downright harmful. Labelling parents as 'hard to reach' feeds into a deficit model of working with parents and has two main effects:

1. It establishes parents as the problem. There's an implied agency here: parents have chosen to be 'hard to reach' and not to engage with the school.
2. It removes the agency for engagement from the school or its staff — it says it's down to parents to engage with school (not the other way around).

One of the main questions we are asked by schools is simply, 'Why won't they engage?' or 'Why won't they come?' School staff often recount a long series of events and interventions, and say that some parents have refused to engage with any of these. We would turn the question on its head and ask, 'Why have none of these things engaged parents?' The difference is subtle, but important. Our question puts the onus for engagement not on the parents but on the event/event organisers.

Every time a family is considered 'hard to reach', think of why that might be the case:

- Look at the list of barriers in Idea 49. Do any of these apply to the parents who are 'hard to reach'?

- Look at the section about how welcoming your school is (Idea 41). Try to think about what coming into the school for the first time would be like for a parent who is scared of school – or perhaps try to remember what it felt like when you came for an interview. Then try to think what would have made it easier. Often just having photos on the website showing what the rooms look like will help anxious parents.
- Ask someone who doesn't know the school to see how easy they would find it to:
  - report a child absent
  - find out when the next field trip is
  - find their way around the school.

All these things can add up to making a school itself 'hard to reach'.

Taking it further

If your school has previously used 'hard to reach' as a label for some parents, think about what you might replace that with that will show a shared agency between school and families.

Don't make parents feel guilty

'I forgot about my son's homework over the weekend but that was because I was tired from a night shift. I felt like my son was told off because of my mistake.'

The world is full of people telling parents they're 'doing it wrong'. Don't add to the chorus.

Think of a child who is struggling to learn something in your class. Which approach works better – telling the child they're not going to learn it and aren't trying, or telling the child you know they can get there, let's try again? (No, we don't think anyone who's chosen to read this book would do the first!) The same applies, as it so often does, to parents – mainly because this is about basic ways of supporting people, not just about learning.

- Whenever possible, start from a positive: 'Your son always manages to make me smile'; 'Your daughter's really supportive of her friends, it's lovely to see'.
- Think before you speak – it's very easy to say things that, given half a chance, we would take back and reframe. Ask yourself: how would you want someone to approach you if it were your child facing an issue?
- Parents may well not be handling a situation the way you would like them to do. Even if you disagree with what they are saying or doing, try to do so in the way you would disagree with a colleague: professionally and respectfully.
- Remember, if you are a parent yourself, it can help the parents of children in your class to hear that you also faced similar struggles and how you overcame them. Self-disclosing in this way doesn't mean that you aren't being professional – merely warm and accessible.

Setting up to support – an iterative process

Part 3

Lead from the top

'Good leadership powers the drive for school improvement and pupils' success.' (Peter Matthews)

Partnerships are more effective, and easier to implement, if senior members of staff are involved and lead on ideas.

One of the things that research has shown for quite a while is that work around parental engagement is much more likely to be successful if it is led from the top – that is, if it has not only the backing but the enthusiastic and active involvement of senior leaders in the school.

You can easily understand why this would be the case, in light of some of the other suggestions we've made, such as the need for a whole-school approach and the need to involve governors. If you are not yet a part of your school's senior leadership team (SLT), here are some suggestions to help get your senior leaders on board:

- Make the case that parental engagement will repay any efforts by improvements in areas of importance to your school, such as attainment, attendance and/or behaviour.
- Ask to have parental engagement as one of your targets – and ask to be mentored by a senior member of staff as you work on your target.
- If you're taking our suggestion to create a reading group (see Idea 94), ask a senior member of staff to be involved.
- Give a member of SLT a copy of this book!

Matthews, P. and Lewis, P. (2009). *How do school leaders successfully lead learning?*. National College for School Leadership (NCSL).

A whole-school approach

'When everyone moves in the same direction, progress is great.'

When it comes to engaging parents, *all* members of staff who come into contact with parents matter.

You'll notice as you read through this book that we usually talk about 'school staff' where you might expect us to mention teachers. This is quite deliberate; if we mean only teachers, we'll say so. Otherwise, we really do mean *all* staff. Anyone who comes into contact with family members needs to understand the value and meaning of parental engagement with children's learning.

There are advantages to this idea: often, teachers don't live in the area where they teach, but the chances are high that other members of staff do live locally. These staff members can be your ambassadors with the local community.

- As far as possible, include all staff in training and discussions about parental engagement, especially front line (reception) staff. These members of staff are often the people parents interact with first and most; it's important that they are supported to do their jobs as well as they can.
- If not everyone can come to the training, make the information available to them and find a way to support their understanding of the value of parental engagement.
- Look at the list of employees in the school and, next to each name/role, note how and when they might interact with parents, and what support they might need to do that well/better. Check this list with staff.
- Remember that your governing body has an important role to play here – include the governors as much as you can.

Teaching tip

While we're suggesting that supporting parental engagement is everyone's job, no one in school has time to do a job someone else is already doing – it's important for there to be central records of what is being done and for these to be accessible to everyone, to avoid duplication.

A wish list for partnership

'What do you believe in as practitioners? What drives you? What do you care about and why?'

To ask someone for directions, you have to know where you want to go. The same is true of initiatives in school — you have to know where you're hoping to end up.

To define your vision for supporting parental engagement, create a wish list, with SMART targets: Specific, Measurable, Assignable (that is, you know who is responsible), Realistic and Time-limited. So, saying, 'Engage with parents more' is not particularly helpful; saying, 'Every pupil in Year 3 to receive a positive text home in term one' is much better. This is specific (positive contact), measurable (contacts might be entered into the Management Information System (MIS) database), it's assigned to a group of staff, it's realistic, and it's time-limited (a term).

Here are some guidelines for creating the specific wish list:

- The initial creation of the wish list is best done as a group activity — perhaps as part of a training session looking at parental engagement.
- It's important that the wish list is owned by everyone; it might start out as the project of a few people, but it should be the shared wishes of staff, parents and families.
- Make sure that the wish list is posted somewhere prominent, otherwise it will fade in importance.
- Set times to revisit and update the wish list into the school calendar.
- Don't forget to celebrate when you accomplish something on the list — and share the celebration with parents and families!

Getting it right for your school

'Sometimes schools need permission to adapt existing advice to make it work in their particular school. Moulding good ideas to take account of a particular context is common sense.'

You're used to adapting resources for teaching – engaging parents is no different!

Although there are lots of suggestions and tips for interventions and ideas for things to do throughout this book, we want to emphasise the importance of process in this whole, well, process.

One of the problems we've found in our work with schools is a lack of joined-up thinking. Everyone agrees it's really important to be doing something to support parents' engagement with their children's learning, but it's also important to do the right thing for your school, your pupils and your families. Not everything will be the right thing – and by 'right' here we mean effective, useful and helpful, rather than the most fashionable, most trendy or most often mentioned on Twitter – so you need to adapt and be selective.

- Talk to colleagues from other schools with intakes like yours: what do they recommend? How have they overcome any barriers faced by families in schools?
- Equally important: what has not worked for them – and why? Is this also something to avoid in your school?
- Gauge the effectiveness of what you're already doing with parents (see Idea 36), and stop doing the things that aren't working!
- Go back to the barriers you identified earlier (see Idea 9). Make sure any new interventions or ideas aren't going to run up against barriers you can't overcome.

Teaching tip

See the online resources for a list of resources that can help.

Taking it further

Be patient: new initiatives can take a while to catch on. You'll have to judge, in each instance, between 'this is not working', and 'this is not working yet'. Further, there's a balance between doing things that are tried and tested, and being innovative. This is, again, something you will have to judge in each situation.

Articulating your values

'No edifice is stronger than its foundations.'

The values you — individually, as a member of a school staff — espouse are the foundation for the rest of your work in school. The values of the whole staff and all of the children underpin all the work in the school.

Many schools will have lists of shared values displayed in prominent places, perhaps as a mission statement. A lot of work has usually gone into the creation of these statements. It's important that these values encourage parents to feel part of the school and of the children's learning.

- Go back to your school's list of values — your mission statement. Does it mention parents or families?
- If parents are mentioned, are they seen as active in relation to children's learning or as passive recipients of information or knowledge?
- Revisit the process of creating a list of values (or a mission statement) but this time, focus particularly on working with parents.
- Ensure that every statement is active, is an action statement.
- Then, treat the statements as the first part of if/then statements — showing the consequences of your beliefs in action. For example:
  - *If* we believe in partnership with parents, *then* we include them when setting targets for children's learning.
  - *If* we believe that learning happens outside of school as well as in it, *then* we have homework policies that support the active involvement of family members.

Good now, even better if...

'Most schools are already working with their parents and families and many are doing great work; you're never starting from scratch.'

You're very likely, as a school, to already be working with parents. However, if you're reading this book, the chances are that you'd like this work to be better, more effective and more useful for families. That means examining what's already going on, and using it as a base from which to build.

During our work with schools, we have found that often one member of staff won't know about the very good work that's going on in other classrooms. Not only is this wasteful of time and effort, it's confusing for parents, as attitudes and practices may then change as their children move through the school. A coherent and consistent approach adopted through the whole school will pay dividends.

- Dedicate a staff meeting or INSET to cataloguing what is already happening in work with parents – create a board in the staffroom that focuses on family partnership.
- Think about what's good and what could be improved (make this an active list accessible to staff in the staffroom). You could also have a space in a public area that parents can contribute to or a parent comment box in the front reception area.
- Share your ideas with a neighbouring school – learn from each other.
- Think about what you want to continue, what you want to tweak, what you want to start doing that you're not doing now.
- Note anything that is being duplicated: how can this be streamlined?
- Don't be afraid to stop doing things that aren't working – no one has time for that!

Teaching tip

In the online resources for this book, you'll find a form called, 'Even better if' that will help.

Taking it further

Ensure you share any parent partnership work that has been successful in a newsletter home to parents. Flag the school's desire to build on and improve partnership and the fact that you welcome input from parents.

The teaching and learning policy

'We created a curriculum that embedded a role for parents and families. Parents could clearly see what the children needed to know each term, and were happy to receive suggestions about what they could do at home to boost their child's learning.'

If parental engagement with learning is going to be at the heart of the school's work and vision, it's also got to be at the heart of the school's policies.

Taking it further

Apply the mind map technique to *all* policies that could/should include parents – Behaviour, Homework, Uniform, etc.

As we've said, the whole point of schools is to support learning. This means that the teaching and learning policy is at the heart of the very reason that schools exist. If we really want to narrow the gap and support all of our pupils, then the teaching and learning policy needs to reflect the importance of parental engagement in children's learning.

- Parents are not peripheral to children's learning and so should not be added on to the teaching and learning policy as a sort of 'extra'.
- Look at all the elements of your policy – where are the opportunities to see learning extended into the home? Where could there be mentions of support for parents?
- Try replacing every mention of 'child', 'pupil', 'staff', 'teacher' or 'parent' with 'person' or 'people'. It's amazing the difference that can make, particularly in policies!
- As part of a staff meeting or Inset day, create a mind map of what you as a school expect parents to do. Consider:
  - Are any of these things active, or are parents and families simply recipients of what the school dictates?
  - Where families are passive, is there a way to make them active partners in learning?

ROIDH – Records Or It Didn't Happen

'The only way to know how to make the future better is to understand the past...'

Our title for this idea is based on the internet abbreviation 'POIDH' (Pictures Or It Didn't Happen). The point is that if you don't keep good, useful records of your work around parental engagement, how can you expect to learn from what's already happened and make things better in the future?

In this idea, we're talking about records of events for parents and families; in the next idea, we'll consider records for communication.

It's important, first, that your records are fit for purpose. They don't need to be overly complex – rather, they need to be *useful* (which they won't be, if they're too complex), and they need to be used and useable, at all stages: planning, during and after the event or intervention. The records need to be stored centrally, where all appropriate staff have access to them.

We suggest that, before any event, the records need to contain the following:

- Title of the event
- Date/duration
- Target audience, e.g. all parents, parents of a particular year group
- The aim/objective: what do you want to accomplish with this event? This is a vital and often neglected bit of planning. What is the aim for parents, staff and, ultimately, pupils?
- Evaluation markers: how will you know if you have accomplished your aims?
- Staff responsible for the event, with contact details
- Resources needed/used.

Teaching tip

A sample template can be found in the online resources that accompany this book. For records you could create after the event, please see Idea 36 on evaluation.

Evaluation, evaluation, evaluation

'Without evaluating an event, how will you know if it's had any impact, and whether it's worth repeating?'

We know that schools are very good at innovation, but it's easy to forget to evaluate the impact of any given event or intervention. Use this idea to help you reflect on an event.

Teaching tip

There is a sample evaluation form in the online resources for this book.

It's important to note that by 'impact' we mean much more than 'parents had a good time' – that's important and can be a good outcome early on in the year or in relationships with parents, but to support children's learning you need to be able to do much more. The main reason for supporting parents is to support the home learning environment – so when you evaluate events, focus on that.

This means, of course, that you'll have to either find ways to evaluate the outcomes yourself or ask parents (or pupils!). This can all be part of the same record system in Idea 35. Immediately after the event, record:

- Who attended? (Use sign in sheets, if you have them, and record the number of people who came.)
- General comments on how it went. (Did the people you targeted attend? Why or why not? How did it go?)
- Even better if... (What would make it better next time? What did you learn from it?)
- Parents' feedback from evaluation forms and oral feedback.

It's important, however, not to stop here. Real evaluation has to take place after a period of time – just as in the classroom, it's not about what pupils can repeat as they leave the classroom, it's about what they've actually learned. It's the same with parental engagement activities – what's important is what's changed, and that change needs to be sustainable and ongoing.

Taking it further

Remember the main aim is about supporting children's learning – that should be the ultimate focus of any evaluation!

- Put a marker in the school calendar six weeks after every event to ask parents to reflect on/ evaluate a previous event.
- You can ask parents and staff the same questions:
  - Do you remember what we did (at this meeting, in this session)?
  - What did you learn, what stayed with you?
  - Can you still see any effects from the intervention?

Be careful about the questions you ask, though – if you ask, 'How good are you at engaging with learning?' our experience is that parents and staff rate this highly at the outset of the journey, and, as they learn more about how much there is to do, the ratings go down, even if engagement has actually increased!

A communications database

'Keeping good records of your communications with parents will save you a great deal of time – and work – in the long run.'

Effective working partnerships with parents are founded on good communication. Schools are remarkably good at giving parents information, as they are required to do, but *giving information is not the same as having a dialogue or communicating.*

We've moved a long way from the days when teachers stood at the front of a class and spouted information. Now, we have a mode of schooling that centres on active learning and communication. We need to make this shift in relation to parents, as well, so that we communicate actively with them.

Most schools keep good records of how to contact parents. You can use that same list for many other things that will also support children's learning. There is no need to create something new; use what you already have.

What we are advocating is a database of communication that school staff have with parents. In whatever way works for you and your school, it's remarkably beneficial if you can keep a record of:

- every time someone contacts home about a problem
- every time someone contacts home with praise for pupils (which also allows you to look at the balance between the two)
- communication over trips, permission slips, sports events
- appointments for parents' evenings
- communication about events aimed at parents and families
- communication *from* parents (communication is two way, remember) and what was done by school staff to follow it up.

Governors on board

'Governors should be at the forefront of helping to establish a culture of parental participation throughout the school.'

If your school has a governing body or board, it's important that those on it understand how important parental engagement is to children's success.

Governors are often left out of discussions around parental engagement. But they are vital to these discussions, as they approve changes to policies and sign off on expenditure; they may also have a say on financing for staff training. Governors are responsible for the performance management of headteachers. Moreover, they'll have to answer questions from Ofsted on all aspects of the school, including engagement with parents.

Here are some steps to help make sure they are well equipped to do this:

- Ensure your governors understand what effective parental engagement is and how to support it.
- Invite governors to any (and all) staff training around parental engagement.
- Offer to attend a governors' meeting to explain what parental engagement in learning is, why it's important and what you are doing about it.
- If teaching staff attend training outside the school, suggest that a governor go along as well.
- Have parental engagement with learning as a standing item on the governing body agenda. Suggest that they add this as an area to be explored when they are hiring new staff.

Teaching tip

There are links in the online resources which will provide help about how to support governors.

Taking it further

If your governing body has governors responsible for specific areas, suggest that someone take on responsibility for parental engagement as their role.

Utilising key members of the community

'Don't try to go it alone; it isn't possible and it's unnecessary.'

Most communities have people right at the heart of them in the form of community leaders, workers and others who, when 'out and about', are known to most of the community. They may be religious leaders, business leaders, people in authority running community activities or centres, or even well-known grandparents.

Who the key members of a community are varies from one place to another. However, if your school has families that come from a tight-knit community, an effective way of building bridges with them is to invite in key figures who are already respected and/or influential among parents and families. Better still, go out to meet them.

The school can act as a central part of the community in this way, bringing people together and making connections. These key figures will also hold invaluable information about community values, expectations and issues that might arise. Try these ways forward:

- Consider inviting key community figures to be governors at the school.
- Try to draw a map – or mind map – of the community in which your school lives. Show the various groups (faith groups, choirs, sports clubs, park runs, etc.).
- See how the groups overlap and interact – in terms of geography (being in the same places) and people (being a member of more than one group).
- Include parents and teachers when looking at group membership.

Being
approachable

Part 4

Making teachers less scary

'But I *am* approachable, they can contact me through the school anytime.'

There is often a gulf between the backgrounds of parents and teachers, which means that making connections with school staff can seem daunting for some families.

Teaching tip

Don't share personal information about school staff, such as phone numbers or personal email addresses, without checking with that person first.

Parents have reported feeling intimidated by teachers. While teachers themselves may not feel this way, it's very important to support to partnership working by ensuring that teachers not only are approachable but also *appear* to be approachable. Teachers often come from very different backgrounds to the families they support, which may mean extra effort will be needed to show you are genuinely approachable.

- Parents need to know that teachers have their own stories to tell. Don't be afraid of sharing your talents, experiences and achievements with parents and pupils. In one school we know, a member of staff told their story of being adopted at a young age – and it was really appreciated.
- Ask staff to contribute to a list of links they already have with the local community. This could be membership of a sports club or choir, for example. Utilise this list to reach out to community groups and to strengthen connections with the school.
- Ask staff and parents to wear clear, readable name tags at events, and add a line to the tag that says, 'Ask me about...'; people can add a hobby, interest or the subject they teach, e.g. 'I'm Mr Jones, ask me about history' or 'I'm Miss Carey, ask me about car repairs'.

- Consider having this sort of information as a permanent feature of the school website.
- Have blank tags and pens so that parents can make their own tags!
- Consider 'highlighting' one staff member at a time in the school newsletter – and include information that goes beyond the school gates. It shows that teachers are human, too!
- Many parents find it easier to approach one teacher than to break in on a conversation two teachers are already having. One school we worked with asked teachers not to stand together on the playground, and found that parents approached teachers more often as a result.

Bonus idea ★

Building parent-staff rapport can be a fun exercise and form part of school fundraising activities. We saw a school quiz with a section on 'When we were young', where parents had to match the baby photo to the teacher!

First impressions count

'Start as you mean to go on!'

Ahead of the first day back to school, if you are a classroom teacher, send a letter or even create a video clip introducing yourself to the parents of your new class.

Parents' impressions of school – and of the schools' opinion of them as parents – and how the school will work with them start forming from the very first moment of contact, whether that's in person, online or in a letter.

Before children arrive for the first time, don't be afraid to tell parents a little bit about yourself, e.g. how long you have been a teacher, what you love about working in this school and any favourite interests. Remember, some parents will easily feel intimidated, so finding ways of connecting with them from the beginning can only help in the long run. Being a down-to-earth professional means that parents are more likely to trust and cooperate with you and the school moving forward. Here are some first impressions to consider:

- What message does your website give about how parent partnership is valued at the school? Is there is a parent portal? (See Idea 97.)
- Think about the journey of parents into the school. Ask current parents about what would make them feel more welcome as they come in; even signs saying, 'Welcome' in a variety of languages can be effective.
- Pay particular attention to the very first day of school. Some parents will be feeling particularly anxious and worried about the transition. It isn't easy handing over your child to a teacher who is unknown to you. There are lots of things you can do to ease this transition for both pupil and parent. (See Idea 66.)

Be friendly to dogs (and rabbits, and guinea pigs)

'Children exist in a complex web of relationships – and that includes the family pet!'

Children, and young children in particular, do not exist in isolation. And that means that they don't arrive at school, or into the classroom, without bringing in at least some of that external environment. You can use this to your advantage.

As a teacher, you know how much that external environment can impact on learning. But the impact can go the other way, and to good effect, so that the learning you're supporting in the classroom can be supported by that environment. Here are some pointers:

Teaching tip

If your school holds a sponsored walk of some kind, make sure families are allowed to bring their doggies along!

- Make sure all relevant staff know about changes to children's home lives that can impact on their learning. This may mean ensuring that all appropriate staff have access to the MIS system, for example.
- Take time in staff meetings to discuss outside issues that can impact on learning.
- The title of this idea recognises that not all the important actors in a child's life may be humans. Showing an interest in a family pet may be the icebreaker that will begin to build a bridge with a family.
- This is another area where it's useful to share information about staff. Consider making a map/mind map of teachers' pets (Who has a dog? A cat? Another kind of pet?) and mirroring that with a map of families' pets. Are there similarities?
- Have large sheets of paper on a wall at parents' evening, for example, asking parents to 'Tell us about your pet!' or 'Who has a dog?' 'A cat?' and so on – this would work best if already populated by staff with their own pets.

Make information easy to find

'I can't find the right information on the website and when it does appear, it is often out of date. I don't have time to call the school office and ask.'

If we want to be able to communicate with parents, the lines of communication have to be open and easy to use.

Although we make the case that you need to *communicate* with parents, not just give them information, there is still a lot of information parents need. Make sure it's easy for them to find and use:

- Ensure that school email accounts are checked regularly.
- Try to avoid a long list of choices on the school phone line – one or two choices are sufficient before the caller goes through to a person.
- Make it clear who should be contacted in different circumstances (absence, sickness, queries about homework, bullying, extra support). Have this information included somewhere obvious on the school website, and include it in newsletters as a matter of course.
- Give parents reasonable expectations for responses to their emails or phone calls. It's easy to forget that just because communication *can* be instant, it may not *be* instant. Let parents know that you will respond to queries within two working days (and be sure you do!).
- Sometimes, you won't be able to answer things directly. If that is the case, let parents know that you have heard their idea or concern and are working on it (within a stated time frame). Sometimes, parents just need to know that they've been heard, even if the answer isn't immediately forthcoming.

Opening the school gates

'"I can't get parents to come through the gate into school!" Our response: "Open the gate and step outside to them instead".'

If we want parents to feel welcome in school, then we have to make the school a welcoming place.

Since you go there so often, it's easy to forget that for some parents, even the smallest, community-orientated primary school can be a forbidding and frightening place. When we suggest you 'open up the school gates' we mean this both literally and figuratively.

- Try to look at your school from the outside, as though you were approaching it for the first time, and as though the idea of doing so scared you. What do you see?
- What simple changes could be made to make it more welcoming? These could be as simple as a welcome mat or sign.
- Once parents are in the school, is it clear where they should go? It helps to have a map prominently displayed so parents don't get lost on the way to 'the bunny classroom'!
- Try to ensure any training includes reception staff as they are often the first members of staff parents encounter.
- Rather than the first sign that parents see being: 'All verbal abuse against staff will be reported', try: 'Thanks for waiting patiently!'.
- Is it easy for those with limited mobility to get around the school? What about wheelchair users, or parents with pushchairs? Can access be made easier?
- Encourage parents of pre-school children into the school so they become familiar with the school environment. Perhaps the school can offer a 'stay and play' session.

Teaching tip

If the school becomes a hub for the community, parents will be more comfortable coming in – that helps to build bridges, relationships and trust.

Bonus idea ★

Some schools have allowed parents space and supplies to start their own 'coffee klatch' groups for mutual support. 'Knit and natter' or 'sit and sew' – or other craft – groups can be a lifeline for isolated parents, so if you have space, offer to host a group.

Host school events away from school

'The school put on a talk in the village hall. Everyone came because it's a place we're so used to going to.'

If parental engagement for learning can happen anywhere, don't confine support for it to the school buildings.

School life tends to centre around the school, and rightly so. We even get into the habit of personifying it: 'The school thinks...', 'This year, the school will...'. This means that 'the school' is much more than the buildings – and is not in essence tied to those buildings. 'The school' can exist anywhere – and probably should.

We've pointed out that some parents may be somewhere between reluctant and unable to come into school – but this doesn't mean that they can't engage with learning. Nor does it mean that they don't deserve your support to do so.

- Think about your local area – are there places you could use for workshops or meetings?
- Ask parents where they think you could have such events. They are likely to know, and possibly have contacts that could help arrange access.
- Some large supermarkets have community rooms – it's worth asking if they would be available for your use.
- Having events outside of school allows you to build the bridges that may lead to parents coming into school – and allows the community itself to learn more about the school and its work.
- Remember to consider transport issues and costs. For example, if you're using a local supermarket, is there a weekly free bus that goes by your parents' homes?

Bring a friend along

'I felt OK attending parents' evening because I was able to bring my Nan with me.'

It's often easier to do things with a friend – and that applies to parents, too.

One thing we've noticed ourselves as parents – and we know we share this with lots of others – is how rarely you are alone in those first years. You get very used to having other people around – so doing something on your own can seem even more daunting than before the child(ren) came along. When that something is going somewhere that makes you feel vulnerable in the first place, it's even harder.

We've found in the course of our research that parents supporting parents can be a very powerful thing (see Idea 88).

- Ask parents who are already coming into school to 'bring a friend along' to every event, if they can/wish to.
- Unless space is very tight, extend all invitations to 'parents and friends' or 'parents and other adult family members'.
- Let grandparents know that they are always welcome at parents' evenings to sit in on the chat, if parents agree.

This suggestion will be most useful and practical for things like workshops or parents' evenings. It might not work for events that are already crowded such as a Christmas concert (but sports day, if held outside, would be a very good candidate!).

Teaching tip

Always remember to check your safeguarding policy when inviting adults into school.

Let parents see what goes on in the classroom

'I would love to know what my child is getting up to in class.'

Thinking outside the box can be remarkably useful!

This is an idea – or a set of ideas – about how to let people who don't/won't/can't come into school know what goes on in classrooms. It's based on an idea from a school we worked with years ago: they had a group of parents who were unable to come into school, but were very interested in their children's learning. So the school, with help from a local business, set up a laptop in the local supermarket. The laptop showed a continuous loop of a lesson (filmed with all the proper permissions). Here are some key lessons we learned as a result:

- Children loved showing their families what they did during the day.
- Parents and families thought it was great because they got a glimpse of their children interacting in school that they might otherwise not get. In other projects, too, parents have told us how important it is to see what happens in the classroom, to know how much teachers really do care about their children. This is a great way to show those relationships in practice.
- The supermarket liked the idea as well, as it increased their footfall, with parents bringing friends and family in to see the lesson video.

You don't need to use that specific idea but, as we've said before, teachers are very good at adapting things to fit their own situations. How else might the idea be used? You could use electronic display boards in your school's lobby or place that parents often frequent to do the same job.

Home visits

'I dress casually and ask them not to bother tidying up.'

Home visits by staff can be a very powerful means of forging relationships between families and staff.

It used to be that almost every child would have a home visit from school staff before their first day in formal education. While the practice has fallen off in recent years, it's clear from research and practice that such visits can be hugely effective. Parents get to know staff in a place they are, quite literally, at home. This affects the power dynamic and helps set parents on an equal footing with staff.

- Try and convey that home visits are the first step in building partnerships; they aren't parenting inspections.
- It's important to let parents know *why* you would like to visit – emphasise that you want to work with them! Parents might worry that you will judge their home and circumstances.
- Plan carefully: you need enough staffing (visits are best carried out in pairs), enough time, and a clear schedule.
- Let parents have plenty of notice and offer a number of options for the time of the visits.
- Text parents a day or two before the visit to ensure they remember you're coming. Keep a friendly tone: 'I'm really looking forward to meeting you tomorrow. Thanks for letting me come along. I'll bring the biscuits!'
- Try to use this opportunity to explain how parents can really boost children's learning and don't need to be teachers to do so!
- If relevant, refer to homework; why you might set it and how parents can help.
- Make sure parents are given an opportunity to ask questions about the home visit before and after.

Teaching tip

For some parents, home visits might be painfully reminiscent of visits from authority figures in the past. Be mindful of this.

Taking it further

Bring along things to do with the child on the visit; the closer these activities are to what goes on in school, the better. Plan things that the parents can continue to do after you leave – literacy games or maths games for older children, playdough for the youngest.

Overcoming and rethinking common barriers

'Barriers shouldn't be blockages – they can be overcome.'

We've often found that when school staff refer to barriers to parental engagement, it essentially comes down to blaming parents. In this idea, we'd like to examine a few of those 'common barriers' we often hear about and suggest some ways to address (or overcome) them.

'Parents aren't interested.'

- While this may be true for some parents, our experience and research literature suggest that most parents are very interested in their children's learning. Many parents, however, may not be interested in interacting with the school – the two are not the same.
- Let parents know how important their engagement with learning is – it can account for up to 80 per cent of the difference in achievement between pupils from different backgrounds.
- For things which have to take place in school, ask the child to create the invitation. One school we worked with helped children write invitations for their parents, then sent home photos of the children with the invitations – and then used these as a background for parents to add their own comments after the event.

'Parents won't come in – they never come in.'

- The first thing to note here is that it's not essential that they *do* come in, and some parents never will come in, but that doesn't mean they can't support learning in the home.
- Have you asked why parents aren't coming in? (This question is best asked after a

relationship has been built up, so that it can be received as a genuine question, rather than an accusation.) You can also ask parents who do attend regularly their views on why others might not want to.

- Have events, workshops, etc. at places other than the school, as we suggest in Idea 45.

'Parents can't help with learning, they don't have the skills.'

- Would you say this about a child in your class: 'She'll not be able to learn this, she doesn't have the skills'? You'd put a 'yet' at the end of that sentence...
- Parents are not, for the most part, professional teachers and we're not suggesting that they should take the place of school staff. Parents don't need those skills so it's not surprising that most don't have them.
- Parents don't need your skill set but they do need skills to support learning in the home – which they've been doing since their child's youngest days.
- If there are specific skills you'd like parents to have – such as how best to support reading and early writing – consider how you can communicate those skills to parents.
- Giving parents a toolbox, for example around key tasks such as helping their child to read, is a worthwhile thing to do. Something like a simple video clip modelling what to do if your child struggles with a word can make all the difference to parents. Model to parents what is optimal and then they will find their own way.

Don't create new barriers

'Schools themselves can, unwittingly, add barriers for parents.'

When planning activities to encourage parental engagement, part of your planning needs to be a check that you're not inadvertently setting up barriers yourself.

Offering something parents don't want in the first place is a sure way to set yourself up for failure. So is offering things at a time or place that parents can't attend, or offering something that won't actually impact on children's learning.

- **Wrong place:** some parents can't or won't come to the school site, so consider having at least some events, preferably early in the school year, somewhere else.
- **Wrong time:** find out what times will and won't work for your parents. If you invite them in for an evening event, try to put on some sort of catering. Find out when your parents celebrate religious events and work around them. Find out if any of your parents work shifts and see what you can do to accommodate them. (Remember that a single parent missing a shift may be losing a substantial part of their income.)
- **Wrong thing:** you wouldn't plan a term's teaching without knowing what pupils need to learn, so why would you plan events for parents without knowing what it is parents want or need?
- **Wrong impression:** sometimes a change of name can be really important. One school moved from having 'Support for maths' evenings to 'I have a teenager, get me out of here' evenings (though the content remained mostly the same). Another school changed their annual BBQ to an annual picnic to increase attendance among vegetarian parents.

Language barriers

'Saying hello to parents in their language shows that you care about, respect and value their cultural heritage.'

Overcoming barriers to do with languages can be an important part of any parental engagement strategy. Many parents of children in your school may have a language other than English as their first language. However, language barriers need not be insurmountable.

A difference in language can often denote a difference in culture. For example, the words for 'house' and 'home' are the same in Polish, so if you are making a differentiation between these concepts, some parents might not understand. Other concepts that exist in one language don't exist in English – ask an Italian-speaking parent or colleague to translate 'simpatico' to see what we mean!

- Many smartphones and some apps for communicating with parents have the facility to translate text/texts from one language to another.
- Have events or displays specifically designed to celebrate the diversity within your school.
- Ask parents in to talk to staff and children about their languages and cultures.
- If you have a variety of languages spoken in the school, ask parents to help you compile a list of common phrases, such as 'Good morning!' to prominently display in the school.
- Ask parents and children to help you compile a set of signs for the school – 'Welcome', 'Reception' and so on, in their own languages.
- Ask parents to become language ambassadors for other parents, offering to translate key information for them.

Bonus idea ★

Once you have the list of common phrases, you can ask parents to help you pronounce things correctly.

Are you helping or hindering?

'We read the school report but it was all gobbledygook!'

When talking to parents about engaging in children's learning, try to avoid jargon and communicate in a way that is easy to understand.

In one secondary school we work with, a parent (taking our advice) asked the maths teacher what her son was doing that week. She received this response by email:

'Your son has just been solving multi-step calculations by prioritising functions according to BIDMAS. He will be moving on to tabulating systemically the information in a problem or puzzle; identifying and recording the steps or calculations needed to solve it and using symbols where appropriate.'

Most parents wouldn't understand much of that information, let alone be able to use it to help their child at home.

We suggest you do the following:

- Discuss with your colleagues the information that was sent to this parent. Do you ever convey information to parents in this way?
- Talk to colleagues about 'translating' key concepts into parent-friendly terms.
- Remember that it is almost always easier for parents to understand if something is modelled to them. Technology can assist – for example, schools can make video clips showing how they teach long division or multiplication. These could be posted on the school website.
- Always tell parents that if they don't understand something that is written in a school report or said to them as part of a conversation, they should always ask for clarification!

Difficult conversations

'Are you sitting comfortably?'

Difficult conversations with parents are a fact of life. They are easier to deal with if they are carefully planned.

Sooner or later, you're going to have to tell a parent something they don't want to hear. We're not suggesting that you avoid those conversations; in fact, situations are often easier to resolve when they are tackled early rather than left to get worse. We do have some suggestions about how to make the conversations go as well as possible:

- Choosing an appropriate place is key, particularly if you are delivering some difficult news or preparing for a trickier conversation. It gives the impression that the conversation matters to you and that you have taken the time to find a suitable room. Offer refreshments or something to nibble on together while you chat.
- Try and ensure that parents can talk to you in private. Often conversations are inhibited because parents are conscious of being overheard or seen talking to you by other parents.
- Have some tissues handy just in case.
- Ask the parent if they are comfortable – this shows that you care about their needs. Before you dive headfirst into the conversation, build up a bit of rapport talking about something light-hearted or non-school related. In short, put them at ease.
- Consider sitting alongside, rather than across from parents.

Teaching tip

Consider using the 3D model for conversations (see Idea 54).

Taking it further

As a rule of thumb, remember that simply giving negative feedback to parents about their child, without any tips for how to improve the situation, can only frustrate and antagonise the parents. You wouldn't do this with a child; you'd have suggestions about how to move forward. Have some suggestions about how parents can shape and influence the situation from their end.

Use a roadmap for difficult conversations

'I used to be scared of difficult conversations with parents but the 3D model gave me the confidence to start the chat and the understanding of how to successfully end it.'

Some conversations are better if they are planned. The 3D model for conversation can come in handy here. It was initially created by teacher educators from the University of Hertfordshire to add structure to improve the effectiveness of professional conversations with colleagues.

The 3D model is also helpful when having professional conversations at work with colleagues. Instead of quick chats over a coffee, more meaningful and purposeful chats are possible!

In any conversation with a parent, remember to watch your and their body language. Listening is an active process so be aware of what the parent is saying and how they are responding.

Using the 3D model, the conversation follows three parts: Discover, Deepen and Do (hence the title 3D). Here's how the model can be used in planned conversations with parents:

- Start the conversation with a **discovery**, mapping it out with the parent, exploring what you both feel the meeting's purpose is, and what you need to discuss. You might use conversation starters: 'Why did you think we needed to meet today?' or 'Tell me how you feel your child is getting on'.
- As the conversation continues, move into the **deeper** part of the conversation where you might probe for more information with prompts such as: 'Tell me more...' or 'I can see you seem quite worried, can you say why?'
- The final part of the conversation ends with action points for both parent and teacher, things that both sets of adults are going to **do** to support the child's learning.

Graham, S., Lester, N., & Dickerson, C. (2012). 'Discover – Deepen – Do: a 3D Pedagogical Approach for Developing Newly Qualified Teachers as Professional Learners.' Australian Journal of Teacher Education, 37(9). http://dx.doi.org/10.14221/ajte.2012v37n9.3

Communication styles

Part 5

Giving information ≠ communication

'There are so many pieces of paper that come back from school in my son's bag, I can't keep up with them!'

As a teacher, you know the difference between just giving a pupil information and actually communicating with them. You need to use that same skill with parents.

Partnerships thrive on communication, on discussion, on interaction, on relationships. Sometimes, a simple giving-of-information is appropriate between partners, but what really makes partnerships work is communication. Here are some tips to help you communicate effectively with parent partners:

- Make sure that information comes to parents in the most appropriate form. Don't send a long email when a simple text would suffice.
- When there is information parents need, make sure it goes out in good time – telling parents on Monday morning that equipment or costumes are needed mid-week poses issues for many parents who work full-time.
- Make sure that parents can see quickly if they are receiving information that does not require a response. This can be done by colour coding, e.g. a blue border means 'take note and file', while a red border means 'response required'.
- Make sure that parents know what to expect from their communications with you – how long it typically takes staff to answer an email, for example.
- Make sure information about how to communicate with school staff is easy to find – check that the contact details on the website are up-to-date and prominent.

Keeping parents informed

'Parents lead very busy lives, and keeping track of school events is just one more thing to do – so make it easy for them!'

Sometimes there are things that parents and families simply need to know, rather than enter into a conversation about.

Information overload can sometimes get in the way of effective communication. Use these tips to give information in a considered way.

- Think carefully about what information parents need on a day-to-day basis, what parents need to be told every term, and what parents need to know every so often or on special occasions. It would be a good idea to discuss this prioritising of information with a group of parents.
- Make sure all parents know how they are going to be informed about different things.
- Ensure the day-to-day and often repeated things are clear and easy to find on the website.
- From your audit of carers (see Idea 23), you'll know *how* the majority of parents prefer to receive information. Use their preferred method, but make sure the information is easily found in other ways as well – on the school website, for example, if appropriate.
- Make sure parents know how you will communicate with them in exceptional circumstances, such as the school being closed due to bad weather.

Bonus idea ★

Make it easy for parents to tell you when their contact details change, too. This is another thing that could live on the school website. Have a change of details form that parents can easily find and fill in on the site.

Plans in plain language

'Jargon makes it difficult to understand simple messages.'

While many of us working in and around schools understand terms like Assessment for Learning, Progress 8 and 'levels', these terms may mean very little to parents.

As we've said before, it's important to *communicate* with parents, not just give them information – but communication requires sharing a language.

- Ask parents you know well to proofread letters home or information on the website – do these things make sense? Are they easy to understand?
- Put a glossary on the website that includes school and educational terms, with simple explanations for parents and others.
- Make sure the glossary is updated at least once a year – terms in education change very quickly!
- Ask the children what terms they've been asked to explain by their parents.
- School reports are notorious for being unintelligible to people outside education. Read one of your reports from the point of view of someone who is not a trained teacher – does it make sense? Is it written in plain language? Is the report giving parents a clear idea of how they can help boost their child's learning at home?

Bonus idea ★

Consider making a school podcast with FAQs. Parents can listen to it on the way to work and it is a lot more fun that sifting through a child's schoolbag looking for school correspondence!

FAQ sheets that are easily accessible

'I asked how my daughter was getting on in maths. I didn't understand the answer. I don't get "partitioning"!'

The easier it is to find information – for parents and for other staff – the more likely it is that the information will be used.

Parents in previous research have told us that, while they are very careful about reading everything that comes home from school at the start of the year, by Christmas they are scanning letters and newsletters to see if their child is in trouble or needs equipment, or if something needs to be signed.

The point about giving parents information is to give them the *appropriate* information, at the *right time*, and to have it *available as needed*.

- Have a clear section for parents on the school website.
- Don't just put everything on the website and assume it will all be read.
- Talk to parents about how it would be best to organise the information. Some suggestions for sections might be:
  1. Permission slips for upcoming events
  2. Resources to support learning (by subject)
  3. Resources for different classes/year groups
  4. Information about after school clubs, sports events, concerts, etc.
  5. Contact information (make sure this is up to date and manages expectations: 'We attempt to answer all emails within two working days', for example)
  6. Links to other organisations, e.g. libraries
  7. Summer holiday suggestions.

Teaching tip

Schools are places that are full of an incredible amount of information – information that often changes from year to year, or term to term. Keeping track of all that information is difficult enough for school staff who are immersed in it all day; it's much more difficult for parents who are at least one removed from the source.

Three tips a week

'The school sends us e-tips on helping with homework.'

We're not dead set on the number three, but it does get the point across that partnership with parents is ongoing and needs to be an embedded part of school life!

While the vast majority of parents want to support their child's school-based learning, many also welcome ideas for how to boost learning at home. If you have a newsletter, or a website that parents use, it's worth adding tips for ways to do this.

- It's important to publish these tips on a regular basis so parents know not only where to look, but also when to look for them.
- Keep in mind what you know about your parents. For example, if your parents are familiar with the local library, by all means suggest an outing there, particularly if you can link it to an event. If, however, you know that most of your parents don't use the library or can't get there (or there isn't one local to them), find some other way to suggest they engage with their children's reading.
- Let parents know *why* you're making these suggestions. For example, helping to make a cake can help children's mark making by practising gross motor movements (stirring the batter) and fine motor movements (sprinkling decorations on the top).
- Once you have a good bank of tips, be sure to organise them so parents can choose tips appropriate to the age of their child.
- Link suggestions to the curriculum where you can. Parents will quickly get into the rhythm of talking to their children about schoolwork and begin to see the benefits.

School reports

'I normally just put them in the drawer to be honest.'

School reports remain an important part of school life – make sure they support learning!

Most, if not all, schools still send reports home in one form or another. And often, these reports are such an embedded part of school life that no one stops to think about the fundamentals of the reports – they take up a huge amount of time, but how do they actually support learning?

Teaching tip

There is no point telling a parent that a child is struggling with focus, understanding or confidence without providing some suggestions of ways forward and how the parent can help.

- Parents always want to know how their child is doing at school and often complain that school reports are simply not regular enough. Don't wait until July to let them know their child was misbehaving during the autumn term!
- Use part of a staff meeting to look at school reports from the point of view of a learning resource – are they fit for purpose? Look at accessibility of language and format. Use simple language. Ask some parents to proofread the template.
- Also ask: what do we want to use the school reports for? Are they just for reporting, or can they go beyond that? Is it possible to add something about how to support learning to the reports? Parents can really get involved in boosting children's learning if they are enabled to.
- Make a place for parents to respond and be sure to show how you use that information.
- When improvements in the child's learning are needed, suggest what parents can do to support them.

Bonus idea ★

Make school reports available electronically and create hyperlinks with suggestions to useful online videos or resources that allow the parents to support their child moving forward.

You said, we did – closing the feedback loop

'Parents need to know that you value their opinion and will react to their suggestions and input.'

As a teacher, you know how important timely, helpful feedback can be for the children – and it's the same for parents!

Teachers know how important feedback is to the learning process, whether it's formal feedback (such as grades) or more informal feedback (such as a discussion around nascent ideas or ongoing work). The same is true of work with parents. Just as it's important to let pupils see a reaction to their efforts, it's important to let parents know that their suggestions have received due consideration and been acted upon if at all possible.

- Elicit ideas from parents in lots of different ways, e.g. suggestion boxes at events, a dedicated email address (suggestions@ yourschool.sch.uk), a section on the website seeking feedback.
- Have a 'You said, we did' board to show how responsive the school is to parent input. This could be around themed ideas, such as: What should our new uniform look like? How should we use the off-timetable time this summer? What can we do to improve our reporting? What would you like to know from the school?
- Display this information where it can be seen: on the website, in newsletters, on a poster board or white board at school.
- In announcing new initiatives, let parents know their origin. Have the initiatives come from the local authority, from another school – or from parents, families or children?

Not all bad all of the time

'When they call about something good that he's done, I can't believe it!'

Parents need to know the good things about their children, as well as any problems.

In thinking about how we communicate with parents, it's worth thinking about *what* we communicate as well. If parents' reaction to seeing the school's number pop up on the phone is an immediate sense of dread, any conversation is off to a bad start.

- Use the communications database suggested in Idea 37 to record not just the times parents are given the bad news, but also the times parents are given good news.
- Commit to telling every parent in your class something good about their child at least once each term.
- It's important to include all the children in this, even the ones who never cause you to phone home with concerns.
- This can be made much easier if you use technology to support your communications with parents. It's very easy to snap a photo of a good piece of work and send a parent a text or email – or to compliment an entire year group or class through a group message. (That doesn't mean that the individual mentions of good behaviour or work aren't necessary, though!)

Playground conversations

'If you have short, regular conversations with parents, it makes any "bigger" conversations a whole lot easier later on.'

Every conversation with a child counts – and so does every conversation with a parent.

It's vitally important for parents to feel they can have easy conversations with staff. The playground is a perfect location for these informal, friendly discussions. Here are some suggestions for how to support those playground conversations:

- Utilise the playground as a visual space. One school we know puts up simple banners showing things like the topic of the week, or 'ask your child to tell you about...', or 'we are looking at __ letter in phonics this week'. This has the advantage, of course, of giving parents support for conversations with their children around learning.
- It's very tempting to catch just a few more minutes to get things done in the classroom, but by being where parents are, e.g. the playground (or wherever they meet their children), you are making it easy for them to approach you.
- If you approach a parent, even just to say hello, be aware that the parent may assume you're the bearer of bad news – a smile goes a long way!
- Use playground conversations as an easy way of passing on the good news about children as suggested in Idea 62.

Bonus idea ★

Have an 'Ask anything' box in the playground so that busy parents can easily slip a note in as they pass through. You may choose to answer these queries in the school newsletter.

Making the most of the school website

'I'm proud of our website, not because it's fancy, but because you can see that we're a school that values parents and is very much a part of the community.'

Your website is the public face of the school – make sure it's what you want people to see!

Often our first encounter with a school is its website – and, as with many first encounters, it leaves something to be desired. While we all know that we shouldn't judge on appearances, when it comes to your website, people – and parents in particular – will do.

- Think carefully about what first impression you want to make with your website – you can't change the façade of the school but you can change the way the school appears online!
- Make sure the website is easy to navigate, otherwise it becomes a source of frustration.
- Many parents will access your website from a mobile phone or tablet. Try to ensure the website is optimised to be seen this way.
- Have a 'Parents and Carers' section – again, clearly marked and clearly indexed. This could contain:
  - news and announcements
  - FAQs to support learning (see Idea 58)
  - copies of letters sent to all parents, and to particular classes/year groups
  - links to relevant policies.
- Consider having a page that clearly introduces staff, including non-teaching staff.
- Having pictures – simple pictures of the school, and what parents are likely to see – will make the website much more accessible and user-friendly.

Bonus idea ★

Think about having a video with a virtual tour of the school on it so parents can familiarise themselves with the school building and the particular classroom that their child will be in during the day (see Idea 83).

Taking it further

It's even better if the children are able to take part in any video presentations about the school – parents are far more willing to engage with material if children are involved!

Helping parents
to help

Part 6

Helping parents to help

'Almost all parents want to do the best they possibly can for their children.'

Parental involvement won't in itself lead to better outcomes for pupils at your school. That is much more likely to arise when the school builds *parental confidence* around helping their children with their learning. When parents understand that they have a contributory and important role to play in their children's learning journey, it makes all the difference.

In earlier sections of this book, we've looked at why supporting parental engagement is a good idea, and how to go about setting things up to make it possible, or increase it, in your school. In this section, we'll give you tips, many of which can be passed on to parents, on *how* to help parents to help their children.

- Prioritise any ideas which fit in with requests or ideas from parents – and don't forget to close the feedback loop, as suggested in Idea 61.
- We don't think anyone would try to do everything we suggest in the space of just one school year, but just in case: don't overload yourself, your colleagues, or your parents.
- As always, pick and choose what's best for you, your school and particularly for your families.
- As always, it's important to:
  - have a plan – how does this fit in with the school calendar? Don't put something on the same week as the Christmas concert!
  - be clear about your aims and objectives and share these with parents
  - know how you're going to evaluate the event or idea before you start
  - make sure you follow up to do the evaluation!

On the first day of school

'The first day of school can be as nerve-wracking for parents as it is for children.'

It is unreasonable to expect immediate parental trust without an articulation of who you are, what you stand for, and how you plan on approaching a year of teaching with their child.

When a parent encourages their child to say hello to you on the first day, it is often with trepidation. What lies at the heart of much parental anxiety is often a lack of knowledge about you as a teaching professional and/or the school. Why would a parent feel comfortable leaving their child in a setting they know relatively little about?

We are not advocating 100 per cent self-disclosure but a little goes a long way. Parents will be more comfortable engaging with a school that applies an honest, transparent and authentic approach to relationships.

- Begin as you mean to go on – this first day can set the tone for so much else; treat parents as partners in their child's learning from the very first day (or before!).
- Let parents know in advance what to expect on that day: How long can they stay with their child? What does the child need to bring? Can parents visit the classroom later in the day to see how things are going?
- Invite parents in and explain what their child will do that day.
- Let parents know that children will likely be very tired and/or excited when they come home – suggest a calming bedtime story.

Bonus idea ★

Video clips of this year's children doing something enjoyable can be very reassuring for parents.

Teaching tip

As always, check policies and permissions before publishing anything that shows individual children (such as videos).

Taking it further

Consider having a blog on the school website that tells parents a bit about Reception and Year One teachers. Augment this with a short video clip if you can, showing parents who will be working with them and their child.

Homework sets the tone

'I dread homework. I don't get why they need so much and when the school does send it home, it stresses us both out.'

Homework, by definition, takes place in the home learning environment. Use it to support parents' engagement with learning.

The debates about the value of homework continue to rage – but we're not going to fan those flames. If your school uses homework, here are some ways that it can be used to help support the home learning environment.

- Is there a better word than 'homework' that you can use?
- Create homework assignments/projects that get parents involved – not just in arts and crafts (though that is important).
- Children could ask parents which books they enjoyed as children and read those.
- Children could ask parents about particular events in their lifetimes. Grandparents, aunts and uncles could get involved too.
- Suggest a walk for parents and children to note down shapes for younger children (e.g. how many triangles can you find?) or new words in environmental print for older children.
- Try to align homework with family life. As soon as homework begins to 'interfere' with family life at weekends, it is a turn-off.
- Suggest questions and prompts that parents can use when their child struggles, gets fed up, etc.
- Tell parents they don't have to sit side by side with their child to help with homework. They can stir the dinner at the same time.
- Help parents see that 'helping with homework' doesn't mean 'doing homework'.

Bonus idea ★

Suggest that children can explain their work to their parents – this is particularly useful in maths, where children may be finding answers in ways that parents don't recognise.

World Book Day (and other events)

'He told me he needed to dress like Harry Potter on Wednesday. I had no time to make him something and instead spent money on an outfit he will wear once!'

Special days are an important part of school life, but be aware of how difficult they can make parents' lives!

Every year, social media is full of wonderful photos of what schools do for World Book Day – but in recent years supermarkets are also full of costumes in the run-up to the day. The same is true for other events and days: Comic Relief, Halloween, Valentine's Day, etc.

Teaching tip

Encourage children to write postcards to their favourite authors for World Book Day, inviting them to write back. It is amazing if/when they get a response.

- Try to find ways of celebrating these special days and events that can involve parents' engagement, but not necessarily parents' wallets – even the outlay of 'a few pounds' is more than many families can afford.
- Dressing up as a favourite character is a great way to celebrate stories, but it's possible to do this at school; over the year(s), collect things that can be used to create costumes in school, on the day.

For World Book Day, consider some things other than dressing up, as well:

- Ask children and families to suggest alternative endings to favourite stories.
- Ask them to come up with storylines for 'The continuing adventures of [their favourite characters]'.
- You might ask parents to spend 20 minutes asking their child about a book they are reading in school. This is a hugely beneficial exercise for children and parents, and costs nothing.

Bath and bedtime games

'Learning can take place at anytime, anywhere...'

As anyone who has had children knows, bath and bedtime with young children can be not only an important time for parent/child interaction, but also more than a bit fraught and difficult!

Teaching tip

It can be useful to share a resource with parents on the importance of sleep for learning.

The following suggestions are ideas to pass on to parents that they can use at bath and bedtime, not only to help set a routine for their child (very important, as you know) but also to support their learning.

- Let the child use shaving cream on the walls of the bath to practise making shapes and letters. This helps with literacy/numeracy and gross motor muscle development.
- Suggest that the child prepare a favourite toy for bed every night, alongside their own preparations – bath, pyjamas, brushing teeth. This helps form routines.
- Make sure the bedtime routine has time for stories, either read from books or told by adults.
- As the child becomes able, let him or her help with reading the stories.
- Try to encourage parents not to let their children fall asleep while using smartphones or tablets! Bad habits start early.
- Remind parents that bath and bedtime is primarily about winding down and not winding up.
- Remind parents that even if their child isn't a fan of reading late at night (perhaps because of fatigue), it is important to do a little reading before bedtime.

Outdoor learning

'Learning doesn't just happen in classrooms!'

Every teacher understands the benefits of outdoor learning for children's development. These days, with time pressures in school and on family life, coupled with the UK's inclement weather, outdoor learning can take a back seat.

There are rich learning opportunities available to children outside when parents and teachers work in a collaborative partnership.

- Try to set homework tasks that involve some outside time, e.g. 'How many mini-beasts can you find under stones in the park?' It isn't onerous, it promotes health and wellbeing, and it's fun!
- Create an outdoor learning hub with other practitioners, with shared resources that can be used for homework or to exchange ideas. In one school, teachers used the village river to conduct some science experiments. Another nearby school did the same and then they compared findings.
- School gardens and vegetable plots provide opportunities for the school community to work together. Inviting parents to help maintain these spaces can help improve teacher-parent communication and enrich mutual understanding. Don't forget to share what your learning objectives are for children so parents understand what you are trying to achieve.
- For families who may not have a garden at home, make sure they know that they can bring in seeds and grow fruits and vegetables for their family's use.

Teaching tip

If outdoor learning is part and parcel of your whole-school parental engagement strategy, all the better!

Taking it further

Outdoor activities should always be linked to learning outcomes and should be part of any curriculum delivery. If you are short of ideas, organisations like The Woodland Trust have downloadable outdoor learning packs! (See the link in the online resources.)

Bonus idea ★

If your school garden needs a boost (perhaps better fencing or equipment), ask pupils to write to the local gardening centre asking for freebies. Perhaps they could sponsor the school veggie plot?

How was your day?

'The question is important, even if you don't get an answer!'

Like many other parents, we both grew very tired of our children telling us they had done 'nothing' all day in school, in spite of all the evidence to the contrary (they were, after all, learning new things). Nevertheless, it is still important to ask the question.

With primary-age children, we understand that parents want to know as much as possible about how their day went. We recommend parents are told to ask, 'How was your day?', but not to bombard children.

In our research with older children at secondary school, young people made it very clear that it was still important that parents kept asking. The correlation we were told was simple, and we heard it again and again: 'If they ask, I know they care'. (This was still the still the case when there was no intention of answering the question!)

Pass on these tips on to parents:

- School is a busy and tiring experience for children. Give children time to relax when they come home.
- Don't bombard them with a barrage of questions about their day. They may need some time just to decompress.
- A simple question asking children to 'rate' their day on a scale of 0–10 where 10 is 'awesome' can work very effectively.
- Parents need to check in with their children, but it should never feel like an interrogation.
- It is important to keep asking, even if children stop responding. It's a way of letting children know you care about their schooling and their learning.

If parents get tired of asking the question and getting no response, suggest these alternatives:

- 'Tell me two things you know now that you didn't know yesterday.' This can even be turned into a family activity, with everyone sharing something they've learned — it promotes conversation and shows parents and other adults are still learning.
- 'What did you like best/least about the day?'
- 'Tell me one good thing, one bad thing, one funny thing and one random thought.' Parents can participate and talk about their daily struggles and successes at work, too.
- 'Who did you eat with today?'
- 'Who did you play with?'
- 'What did you do really well today?'

Bonus idea

Make a list of these alternative questions available for parents on the website, and include this information in the pack given to parents before children start school.

Meeting for a meal

'Eating together can be a powerful leveller and a binding force.'

All too often, staff and parents only encounter each other when time is short (parents' evenings) or when there is a problem to discuss. Sharing a meal, however basic and simple, can help lay the foundations of the trusting relationships that are so essential for partnership working between staff and parents.

As humans, we attach a deep-seated importance to breaking bread together – consider the value we place on the first meal with a new partner's family, or holiday dinners, and how important it can be to gather around a table as a family.

- If you already have a breakfast club, open it to parents, either all the time or on a regular basis.
- Most families have a 'special dish', so organise a shared meal where families can each bring along their favourites. This allows parents to come into school with something worthwhile to share. Depending on your parents, consider having a fund that parents can dip into or a stock of essentials they might use, such as rice and pasta. It is an added bonus in multicultural schools, where events like this can facilitate discussions between people from different cultures about cuisines and menus.
- Institute regular 'Stay and sip' days for school – find a place that parents can stay and have a cup of tea and a biscuit after dropping off their children. This helps to build a community among parents, as well as within the school.
- It's important for staff to participate in these events as well. It all helps to break down barriers and show that staff are people too!

Cook 'n' learn!

'We both work. Cooking and eating together is the most precious time of our day. I would rather talk to my children about their learning while I cook, than sit down to do homework with them after the meal.'

Often parents are unaware of how to embed learning into things like baking or setting the table. With a few easy prompts, they can be reinforcing the work that you've done in the classroom that week.

Whether is it chatting about fractions when they are dividing up the pizza at teatime, weighing out the sugar when baking a cake, or counting the number of knives and forks that need to go on the table at supper time, children can be building up their knowledge and skills at home. It's an easy win.

Emphasise to parents:

- They don't need to be experts in any subject to engage meaningfully with their child's learning.
- They are 'doing the right thing' when they talk to their child about maths or science, for example.
- Asking questions is key to opening up a child's thinking. They do not need to know the answers.
- Parents can simply ask their child to explain something to them or teach them something. That can be hugely beneficial to the child.
- Homework can be completed while a parent is cooking – parents don't need to stand over the shoulder of their children as they do their homework! There are countless ways that literacy, maths or science can be embedded.

Teaching tip

There is a helpful video on family maths within the online resources that you can download and share with parents. It models a parent talking about maths while cooking the tea!

Bonus idea ★

Have an 'our favourite dish' pot luck dinner at school, with each family bringing in their favourite dish. Perhaps the children have to talk about it, explain why the dish is special to their family, detail the ingredients and talk about the process of cooking it!

It all adds up – parents and maths

'I have no idea how to help my child with their maths homework and I wouldn't dare help for fear of getting it wrong.'

Many people feel helpless in relation to maths; we need to support parents to feel powerful.

Teaching tip

There are lots of resources to support parents with maths – many are listed in the online resources for this book.

Many parents struggle with maths, particularly as children grow and move through the school system. While 2 + 2 may not feel overly taxing, fractions may present more of an issue, and quadratic equations may be mind-blowing. We know that many people experience what has been called 'maths anxiety'.

Often, parents recoil from helping with maths homework or even talking about maths, based on their own experiences as pupils themselves. This reaction to maths can be transmitted to children from parents (and teachers!), setting them up for failure rather than success. This needn't be the case, however: helplessness that is learned can be *unlearned*, as well.

Particularly around maths, school staff need to support parents not only to help with learning but also to *believe* that they can help.

- Suggest ways parents can highlight everyday maths to their children – doubling the quantities in a recipe, for example, or adding up items in a shopping basket.
- Many parents who feel they struggle with maths may be able to deal with certain areas of maths, such as those involved in sports league tables. Suggest that they discuss these with their children.

- Try to avoid making maths seem TIRED (Tired, Isolating, Rote learning, Elitist and Depersonalised) and instead make it seem ALIVE (Accessible, Linked, Inclusive, Valued, Engaging).
- Consider some family learning activities that would be enjoyable and include maths, e.g. designing kites or virtual racing cars.
- Advise parents that board games or even playing cards or bingo at home can make a big difference to a child's attitude to maths and how well they begin to perform in mental maths at school.
- Make sure there are FAQs or tip sheets available to parents about calculation strategies, etc.
- Maths can be quite gendered. There are lots of resources to support girls around maths, e.g. posters of famous female mathematicians. See what is available; you may be able to make your own posters cheaply.

Taking it further

Parents' ways of finding the answers to maths problems may be different from the ones children use now, but different does not equal wrong. Let parents know that children need to show that they've used a specific way to find their answers, and that it may be new to them as parents – that's a very different message!

Use effective praise with children

'My child has always been good at spelling. Sometimes I just forget to tell them how well they're doing.'

Parents may not realise how important effective praise is, or know how to deliver it.

All parents want to know how to help keep their child motivated to learn and do well at school. When they realise that the way in which they praise their child can impact on a child's attitude, then they are keen to do 'the right thing'.

Most teachers have heard of Carol Dweck's work on mindset. Dweck helpfully suggests phrases that parents might use that can keep a child motivated and feeling supported. For example, if a child does particularly well in a school assessment, parents might be tempted to say something like: 'You're such a smart boy!' But there's no room for improvement if you're already the best!

Encourage parents to value their child's effort and perseverance in getting there when they give praise:

- Wow, you must have revised those words so well to get such a good mark!
- You're the kind of kid who gets things done.
- You always try your best and I really like that.
- I've noticed you working hard this term and it's paying off.
- You did it! It was a tough job but you stuck to it.
- You are one hard worker, you know that?

Parents' evenings

'Nobody enjoys parents' evenings. We dislike them and many parents don't even bother to come in. What's the point?'

Parents' evening is a unique opportunity to build on your relationship with parents, impart information about children's learning and learn from parents about their child. At its best, it's about working in partnership with parents.

Almost every teacher who has experienced them has asked, 'what is the point of parents' evenings?', in tones of greater or lesser desperation.

Parents' evenings are often used for reporting, or indeed, for repeating reports that have already been sent home. If you think it's time for a change, why not centre parents' evenings around support for learning?

- Ask your children and their parents what they *really want* out of parents' evenings. Ask the same question of staff. Can their suggestions be incorporated into future events?
- Parents often find such events stressful and even intimidating, and sometimes come away without having found out what they wanted to know. Send home a list of questions parents might like to ask you on the night – better still, ask parents beforehand what they want to know.
- Consider having a demonstration lesson (or two) going on during parents' evening. Make it something parents can join in with, such as a cookery lesson, or a discussion of something current. Remember to build in time and space for this.
- Try to avoid using some sort of timer for the slot with parents. There is something off-putting about a teacher slamming a buzzer when you are about to ask a really important question as a parent.

Teaching tip

Refer to parents' evenings by a different name – perhaps 'learning review evenings'.

Bonus idea ★

Have badges that tell parents more than just names, e.g. 'I'm Mrs Jones – ask me about car mechanics!' or 'I'm Mr Smith – ask me about archery!'

Reading together – parents and literacy

'If we can get parents reading to their children and listening to them read at home, we are surely setting them up for life.'

Parents know how important reading is, but they may not know the best ways to support it. This is particularly an issue for early reading skills.

Taking it further

Start a 'What I'm reading at the moment' board for staff and parents, as conversation starters and recommendations.

Parents need to be reminded that, as Ros Wilson would say, 'If they can't say it, they can't write it'. Children who are exposed to lots of chat and language at home are more likely to use language in school essays that is bold, ambitious and expressive. It delights parents to think that they can actually impact on their child's literacy levels simply by talking to them.

- Create a library of resources that families can borrow: flashcards, books, conversation starter packs, story sacks.
- Let parents know how important nursery rhymes and songs can be; have a store of these on the school website.
- Let parents know that setting a good example – letting children see them read and having reading time together as a family – is very important.
- Let parents and children know that you, too, read for pleasure.
- Set homework that encourages the skills of early reading and explain these to parents, such as 'collecting words' when out and about: what new words can they see?
- Open up a classroom, or any accessible venue, for a 'Parents' book club' – or it could be a writing club.
- Sharing stories that teachers may have written when they were little can be a fun way of engaging parents in discussion about

things like creative writing and showing that everyone struggles!

- Let parents know how important discussion and chat are to support reading.
- Invite local authors to come in and work with children, read to/with them, and talk to parents.
- Combine your search for speakers with some literacy activities for children by asking them to write to local celebrities/business people and invite them to give talks at the school. Some of these people will be of great interest to parents and they will welcome the chance to come to the school for reasons other than hearing how their child is getting on. Of course, knowing your parents and their range of interests will help to give you clues as to who might be a crowd pleaser!
- Explain the concept of 'environmental print' to parents – let them know that they don't have to buy lots of expensive books to help their children read!

> **Bonus idea** ★
>
> Contact your local library – see how you can work with them to help families enrol in the library, and let families know what facilities are there.

Look on the bright side

'It's lovely when teachers tell me something nice about him, but it doesn't happen very often!'

Grandma's idea about 'not saying anything unless you can say something nice' has a grain of truth in it. In any conversation with a parent, they will always worry in case you might pass on some negative news about their child, so hearing something positive from a teacher can be a rare treat.

Of course, there are times that parents need to be told things that are difficult to hear or uncomfortable, and that's fine. However, by giving parents positive feedback on how their child is doing, it makes the trickier conversations so much easier next time round; it's worth trying to achieve a bit of a balance.

- Try to make at least one positive phone call, text or letter home per week (to begin with).
- Once you've established a routine, increase this to two or three a week, so every child should have at least one positive message a term.
- Make sure these communications are entered into the record system (see Idea 35).
- Keeping those records will also show who is – and is not – getting the encouragement they may need.
- If parents are only used to hearing from the school when there are problems, they may be defensive when you first phone with good news. Keep going!
- Give parents feedback when and where you can – reading logs are one of the places where there is often at least a weekly exchange between parents and teachers. Give parents a pat on the back here if you can. You might say things like: 'Katy told me you read a lovely story last night – well done Daddy!'

Bonus idea ★

Schools use stamps all the time: Star of the day, Wonderful work, Verbal feedback stamps, to name but a few. What about a 'Terrific support stamp' for mums, dads, grannies and grandpas who do so much night-time storytelling?

Who does what?

'We're not here to raise children, we're here to support parents and supplement the great work that they do at home every day.'

Parents may be children's first and continuing teachers, but that doesn't mean their job is the same as yours.

Some teachers may worry that in supporting parental engagement, there is a danger of diluting their own role. We believe that teachers should help define the roles that parents and schools play in children's development.

- Parents are the child's first and most important teacher.
- You are there as an expert in learning that has to do with the school curriculum.
- Parents have a powerful role in shaping a child's attitudes to learning and overall aspirations.
- Both of you want the child to be happy, motivated to learn and thrive at school. For this to happen, both of you need to be communicating openly with each other, sharing any information that might affect how the child engages with learning, and working together to ensure that the child behaves well at school.

Both of you want the child to thrive academically, too. This is best achieved by an understanding of the 'pass the baton' approach. Parents need to support you when you:

- send homework home
- request information
- discipline their child.

In turn, you can promise to listen to their perspective, be understanding of their situation and committed to encouraging family learning in a way that respects different family circumstances.

Taking it further

At the point of transition into the school, you might send guidance to parents around what your role is, and how it complements theirs. By explaining this explicitly, you can also highlight the fact that if parents want to boost their child's learning at home, there are plenty of things that they can do!

Sharing goals

'Everyone wants the best for the children – we're all in this together!'

Working in partnership with parents means letting them be part of the learning process from start to finish. That includes setting goals.

As a teacher, you know how important it is to set goals for learning (and to celebrate when those goals are achieved). The same is true for your work to support parental engagement – it's important for parents to help set goals for their children, to see if/when they are achieved, and to celebrate good work.

- Share children's learning goals with parents – let parents know what a child is hoping to accomplish or master in the next term.
- Better yet, engage parents in *setting* the goals in the first place, based at least partially on finding out from parents what children can already do, or already know.
- Show parents how learning builds over time, and how they can contribute. For example, almost all parents will think it's important that their children learn how to write, but many may not realise that many forms of play build muscles for the gross and fine motor movements required to write.
- Let parents know simple ways to help achieve goals. In the example above, for example, parents may not realise that playing with playdough can help develop those muscles.
- Ensure that parents join in the celebrations when learning goals are achieved. A simple text or note home will do the trick, if parents are aware of the process from the outset.

'You shall not pass' – fear of the school gate

'When the teacher stands with her clipboard in the playground and talks at me about my son's behaviour, I just don't want to be there.'

For many parents, the school gates present an almost impossible obstacle. Often due to their own experiences of education, many parents feel at best unwelcome and often profoundly anxious if they need to come on to the school site.

Remember that while for you school represents a workplace, for many parents attending a school event can make them revisit unhappy memories. They often don't feel at all at ease, even when they're there to support their children. These feelings can be exacerbated if: the school is the same one they attended as a child; they associate school with failure or unhappiness, e.g. being bullied; the school is entirely new to them, is large and difficult to navigate.

You can't go back and change parents' experience of their own school days. You can, however, give them new, school-related memories that are pleasant, rather than anxiety-producing. The ideas below relate specifically to helping parents feel comfortable coming into school.

- Consider making a short video clip showing parents around your classroom so they feel more at ease dropping their child off on the first day.
- Ensure that all parents have a clear, labelled map of the school, and that these are available in any languages needed by your parents (and use symbols wherever possible). Make sure this is easy to find on the school website as well.

Teaching tip

Refer to Idea 10 and Idea 45 for working with parents off-site.

Taking it further

Consider the decorations and posters parents and others see around the school. Are labels clear? For example, on pupil art work, 'Jenny Jones, Acorn' is OK but 'This painting, done by our pupil Jenny Jones from the Acorn classroom, represents Jenny's take on modern life' is much more informative.

Bonus idea ★

Consider a family treasure or scavenger hunt for new pupils and their families. This can accomplish the same function as a school tour but is much more fun and could have a learning element.

Encourage parents to find out what interests their child

'The teacher told us at parents' evening that James was fascinated by the topic of planets in science. She gave us the names of some places we could take him to over the holidays.'

A child's inclinations towards particular topics or activities can take time to emerge, but teachers' observations about a child's interests can be very helpful to parents. Parents appreciate these observations because it means that you have taken time to get to know their child and it shows that you have their child's best interests at heart.

Teaching tip

Remember that, as a parent, to receive a lovely compliment about your child when you least expect it feels wonderful! This feedback can be another building block in the parent–teacher relationship and makes trickier conversations later on so much easier.

You would expect that parents already know what interests or engages their child's interest, but that isn't *always* the case. Some parents unwittingly impose interests onto children (e.g. decide on ballet for girls, rugby for boys) without really considering what they are naturally drawn towards first.

This is your perfect opportunity to create alignment between home and school. Don't wait until parents' evening or school reporting season to let a parent know that you have seen their child engage wholeheartedly in a particular activity at school. Observations can be made and passed on during playground chats, first thing in the morning at the school gate or even by phone – though try not to call them 'observations' as this sounds rather clinical and scary!

You might use phrases with parents such as:

- I can't believe how much Essen loves a challenge, particularly when we bring the Connect Four® game out in the classroom!
- I love the way that Ellie is completely absorbed in what she's doing when she's drawing. She really engages with it.

- Your son is so engaged and interested when we talk about numbers, he clearly has a natural interest in maths! Have you noticed this?
- Jamil seems so interested when I talk about my puppy in class, is he interested in animals outside of school? Have you got a pet?
- I just wanted to let you know that every-time we had science this week, Goyo was telling everyone in the class about the planets! It's clearly his thing!
- Isha really has a flair for debating. Every-time we have a discussion in class, she is so eloquent!

Once you have initiated conversations with parents highlighting a child's talents and interests, you can start to create some thinking around nurturing those talents. Parents will usually be open to your suggestions but they may need some sign-posting.

> **Bonus idea** ★
>
> Not all parents will have the funds to take their children to activities further afield, so always provide free options, e.g. free admission museums, exhibitions and opportunities that are affordable to all.

Virtual tour of the classroom

'I never knew what my daughter did all day – it's great to find out!'

Not all parents or family members will be able to come into the classroom – but that doesn't mean they have to be excluded from seeing what goes on in school. In this idea, we're suggesting you provide a 'virtual tour' of the classroom, to be uploaded to the school website.

Some parents and family members won't be able to come into classrooms during the day, and some may not be able to come in at all. 'Not coming in' is definitely *not* the same as 'not being interested'.

There are a lot of ways to support parents' engagement with learning that don't require them to come into school, and creating a video tour is an excellent first step.

- Make the creation of the video tour a whole-class activity.
- Be creative with how this can fit in with what pupils are already learning.
- There are obvious links to literacy in writing the scripts and to technology in producing the video.
- Children can also practise their speaking skills by providing the narration for the video.
- They can practise other skills by giving demonstrations as a part of the video. For example, they could show viewers how to use the number line or how to choose a book from the library, or they could even demonstrate a new song or dance the class has learned!

'All about me' letters

'We ask questions because we are excited to discover all about new families joining our community.'

One of the schools we've been working with has instituted what we think is a great new part of children's entry into the school. When children arrive, either at the beginning of term or at any other part of the year, parents are asked to fill in an 'All about me' form.

The idea behind an 'All about me' form is simple: it gives parents – and children, when they are old enough – a chance to tell school staff things they might find it useful to know about their pupils, but might otherwise not find out.

Sometimes this will replicate information held elsewhere, e.g. allergies. At other times, however, it might bring to light entirely new aspects of the child, e.g. 'I'm fascinated by dinosaurs and can distinguish all the most common species. Ask me about dinosaurs!'

Such forms provide two very useful functions. The first, of course, is that they give school staff information about pupils that might not be available to them otherwise, and secondly, but perhaps more importantly, the forms signal to the parents and child that you take families' knowledge about the pupil seriously and want to work in partnership.

- Add an 'All about me' or 'Tell us about your child' form to parents' information packs for new starters.
- Note in your prospectus *why* you want parents to fill in these forms.
- Some schools have asked Year 6 parents to write letters to their own children noting why parents are proud of them.
- Keep up the dialogue that shows you value parents' knowledge of their children, for example at parents' evening.

Teaching tip

You might model an 'All about me' letter by sending one all about you home to parents! For example, 'I'm Miss Jones. I have a cat who likes to help me mark work, and I will be much happier after my first (or third!) cup of tea.'

Avoiding the summer slide

'Don't let all great learning go to waste. Over the summer, parents can help sustain your efforts so pupils aren't starting from scratch in September.'

Learning shouldn't stop in the holidays. When the summer break comes, it's time to pass the learning baton on to parents. A few tips for parents on how they might engage with their children can really help.

Taking it further

Give parents an idea of what you will be covering in class come September and suggest parents talk to their children about those particular topics.

First of all, too few parents are aware of what teachers know too well: that learning takes a dip during the holidays. Yes, children need much deserved rest and relaxation, but there is a need for some upkeep in terms of the learning over the holidays. Parents don't want anything too onerous, just a few tips on how to sustain the great work that you have put in with pupils over the year.

- Suggest that parents and children write postcards to each other, or other families, during the summer – collect these in for a display in the autumn.
- Give parents clear information about what's on for their children over the summer. Many libraries have free events for children throughout the summer, for example. Often local organisations will happily supply the school with the information, so you don't need to do the legwork.
- Include a list of 'free things to do in the area' on the school website, particularly for holiday periods, or let parents know about local activity websites.
- Leisure centres may also offer low cost or free events to families. Try to build a relationship with the marketing department of these places so they keep you regularly informed of children's activities.

- If services exist to ensure that children have meals throughout the holidays, signpost these to all parents.
- When it comes to maths, encourage parents to partake in chat about numbers and numeracy when 'out and about' or when they are together over the holidays. What you are trying to achieve is parents who are aligned with what you are doing in the classroom. For example, if you have been doing fractions in class, remind parents just before the summer to chat about fractions when they are at the beach or cooking and sharing out the pizza.
- Parents aren't normally keen on 'formal' homework during these summer months so keep it nice and easy.
- When it comes to literacy, parents should be encouraged to see the value of conversation and family time with their children over the holidays.
- Encourage parents to stretch children with 'big words' over the summer, collect new words, write about and photograph their experiences over the summer, where possible. Writing tasks should feel easy – sending a postcard to Grandma, compiling a shopping list, reading menus in the café.
- When you come back next year, remember not every child has had a 'good' summer, been away or had a holiday. For some, school is the best part of their lives – be sensitive in how you ask about the summer.

> **Bonus idea** ★
>
> Local libraries often organise summer book clubs that families can participate in. Ask the library to send the school details or invite in a member of the local library to talk about it.

Parent-to-parent work

'Peer coaching is cheap, popular and highly impactful.'

Parent-to-parent support, in the form of workshops, has been shown to be very effective, particularly when parents are relating to others from their own communities.

We all know that sometimes it's easier to go somewhere new with a friend, and easier to relate to someone you know, someone on your own level, than to ask for help from someone you don't know well, someone who might be quite different from you. We know that some teachers come from very different backgrounds to those of the families they work with – this can make it difficult for parents to approach teachers. And that is before you take into account differences in culture and language.

- Consider having some of your parent workshops led by other parents. It may require you to work with the parents and to support them to have the skills necessary – consider this an investment that will bear fruit for a long time.
- The parent survey (see Idea 23) should help you find out who might lead different workshops.
- Be prepared to model learning for the parents – it's very helpful if staff can go along as learners. You'll need to think carefully about this, as it would be very appropriate in some cases (e.g. learning how to make candles for Christmas) and not helpful at all in others (e.g. attending a parents' circle).
- Some members of staff may also be parents and, again, you will need to think carefully about how you present yourself in such situations. You may think you are attending an event as a parent, other parents are still very likely to see you as a teacher!

Sustainable practice

Part 7

What is sustainable practice?

'Engaging parents in learning isn't a one-off event; it needs to become part of "the way we do things".'

Supporting parental engagement with learning needs to be embedded practice. It's not a bolt-on extra.

Other sections of this book cover why engaging parents is important, and give pointers to ways to go about it. If we want support for parents to become a usual, normal part of school life, then it needs to be:

- **practical**: meaning not only 'possible' but 'possible within the constraints of a busy school'
- **effective**: meaning it does what it says on the tin, it supports parental engagement with learning
- **sustainable**: because that's the only way it can really become embedded.

This section looks at how to make those practices sustainable and practical, within the incredibly busy lives teachers and parents already lead. We need to reiterate some points here:

- Don't do things that don't work – or at least, don't keep repeating them.
- Keeping good records will help you decide what does – and does not – work for your parents and families.
- Those records will also help you avoid duplicating work that colleagues are doing.
- Get colleagues together and think about the same issues that keep repeating year on year and that get in the way of effective parent partnerships. What can you change so that things improve rather than stay the same?

Building capacity

'Parental engagement wasn't part of my teacher training – I really wish it had been!'

There is a lot of talk about building capacity within the teaching profession, but it's very rare to hear supporting parental engagement be part of that discussion. However, just as with the other skills and knowledge that make up a teacher's job, supporting parental engagement needs thought, care, reflection and training.

Suggestions are made elsewhere in the book about training around parental engagement – see in particular Ideas 29, 30, 38 and 44.

Here, we are talking about embedding the work of that training.

- Your records are a part of building capacity – not only keeping records of what's been done but also of resources, so that they don't have to be created time and time again.
- When new teachers join the school, make sure that your ideas about the value of parental engagement are part of their induction.
- Take the opportunity to find out what new members of staff know and have done in this area, as well!
- Remember to treat engaging parents in children's learning as an important part of teaching practice, worthy of reflection and thought.

We need to reiterate a couple of further points here:

- Don't go it alone. Work with colleagues, from your own or other schools, as often as possible.
- Don't try to do it all. Pick and choose carefully, in accordance with your aims and objectives.

Teaching tip

Don't neglect the value of other agencies and charities. There's a list of useful contacts in the online resources for the book!

Bonus idea ★

Even subject-based CPD should always include, 'what about home learning?' as a part of the day.

Celebrating successful partnership

'When the head wrote to us and commented on how well we supported our son, I cried!'

Parents like praise too.

We all like to be praised, and we know how important positive praise is for children. How often during the day do you say things like, 'Well done!' 'Good job!'. We also know how important it is to praise effort. But how often do we praise parents?

- If parents have responded well to something you've suggested they do, let them know you appreciate what they've done.
- Let parents know when their child is doing well because of their support.
- Let parents know how important positive praise is to their children.
- Don't forget to praise your colleagues, as well!

Anything that teachers and schools can do to encourage quality family time is worthwhile! When children (and adults) feel that they are doing a good job, they are more likely to keep trying – praise will help everyone feel better about their work.

Creating sustainable resources

'We teachers don't need to reinvent the wheel. Most of the time the material we need is out there already, we just need to locate it.'

There is no point in recreating things year after year if they can be made to serve a long-standing purpose.

Schools are strapped for cash and time; try to create or access resources that can be used year on year, and to use resources that are already available.

Sometimes the things that are available will need to be tweaked a bit for your families – but again, this is a skill you already have and use hundreds of times a year, when you see a good idea and think how it could be used to advantage in the classroom.

Here are some ideas:

Teaching tip

Why use paper when technology will do? Parents may prefer to watch a quick clip on what is coming up this week at school rather than trying to read a long school newsletter!

- Automate everything you can when creating forms. Find out how to use tools in word processing programmes that will do things automatically – changing the date, for instance, or inserting page numbers. This all saves you time.
- The database of resources you build up should be your first stop, rather than creating letters or flyers from scratch each time.
- The same holds for events – your records should show you what worked last time.
- Parents are your best sources of information about what works, so ask them!
- The online resources accompanying this book offer a one-stop shop for links and resources you can add to your database and use time and again.

Involve other agencies, local businesses and community groups

'The local gardening centre ended up supplying us with all the seeds and soil for our new vegetable plot in the playground. They even brought along the first batches of soil!'

To reiterate, don't try to do all this alone! Your school is at the centre of its local community. The very best schools consider themselves hubs for community activity and dialogue.

At every opportunity throughout the school year, take the chance to reach out to others and involve them in the events that take place. It's great for the community and will really benefit your activities and events:

- When you run school competitions, invite local business people in to be the judges at the events. It might even be a local writer or children's author.
- If you are located near a university, write to ask the Vice Chancellor to come along and host your prize-giving day!
- Ask a local artist to judge the school art competition.
- For fundraising activities, you might consider running a baking competition. Can the local baker come and judge the winning entry?
- Poetry competitions and debates are fantastic for developing children's social and speaking skills in general. Invite the editor of the local paper in to judge any school competition or, even better, the Headteacher or Head of English in the biggest secondary school in the area! Children and families may one day meet these important figures and meeting them in fun circumstances can be great for future transition to big school!

Bonus idea ★

While you might have a brilliant PTA who can help organise these events, we think it's even better if children do the asking. Most adults won't say no to an eloquent child at the end of the phone or one who has written them a lovely letter!

Develop relationships with local media outlets

'Parents – and prospective parents – don't just find out about schools through word of mouth. Talk to your local newspaper and radio stations!'

Schools are often so busy doing great things that they forget to tell the world about them! Sure, it might land on your Twitter page but that won't be as effective as landing on the front page of your local paper.

There are several ways in which you can let the local community know what the school is up to:

- Via nearby universities who will all have staff and student portals. Should your school require a speaker for an upcoming event, ask the university to circulate your plea!
- Via your local community radio station. These stations are delighted to promote what is going on at school and even to feature pupils on air! More often than not, they have profiles on social media that your school can connect to. Your school might even sponsor an advert or on-air jingle. Where your school is running a charity event that the public could contribute to, let the station know about it. Sometimes they will allow you to list the event for free on their website.
- Via local event pages. Every town in Britain is now replete with its own network of sites that highlight local attractions and events. They are often happy to receive details of events that the school may be running and where the public are invited.

Teaching tip

Let the community know what is going on at the school. As far as possible, try to encourage local businesses to donate, contribute and have an input into school life.

Taking it further

Celebrating school initiatives, achievements and good news stories in the local press is a fantastic way of ensuring that the school has a positive digital footprint.

This simian belongeth not to me

'You can't do everything, so concentrate on what's important, and on what's in your power to change.'

The title of this idea comes from the Polish saying, 'Not my circus, not my monkey'. Over the years, the phrase has come to mean that not all problems are yours. It's OK to say, 'Not my monkey, not my problem' at times.

This idea gives you permission to say, effectively, that you can't solve everything – and you don't need to try. In all areas of school life, it's important to know one's limits – and also what limits should be in place:

- Teachers often run up against things that they are not trained to deal with. Know what to do when that happens.
- Have handy and easily-accessible lists of agencies and people to contact in different situations. Know when to hand things to others.
- Make this ability to accept there are some things you cannot deal with the subject of staff training. Don't assume that 'everyone knows' – make sure everyone really does know.
- Make the list of contacts and outside agencies available to parents, as well – they may not want to contact the school, for example, to find out how to get help with financial issues (this could go on the website but make sure it's kept up to date!).

Bonus idea ★

You could consider having a community resource page on the school website that signposts families to additional support beyond the school.

Don't reinvent the wheel

'No one has time to do work that's already been done!'

School staff are masters at make-do-and-mend, and at pick-up-and-adapt; don't be afraid to apply the same skills to working with parents.

Believe it or not, if you have an idea about how to engage parents, chances are others have already thought of it or developed a relevant resource!

We understand that many school staff could greet a book like this with dismay: how could you ever implement all these ideas? Remember:

- You don't need to do everything.
- You don't need to do everything at once.
- You don't need to do everything alone.
- You don't need to do everything from scratch.

Parental engagement with children's learning has been an important topic for schools for a long time and there are thousands of books, articles and websites out there with suggestions and ideas. In fact, there are so many that it can become bewildering and off-putting.

- Choose some well-known, well-founded resources as a basis for your work.
- Form a reading group, preferably with staff from more than one school; everyone reads a different article or book or investigates a different resource and reports back. Pool your knowledge.
- Utilise the knowledge of any new members of staff, or if anyone is doing an MA, PhD or EdD, you could suggest that this would make a good topic for a paper (or dissertation).
- Keep good records, particularly of things that you think are useful.

Teaching tip

You'll find hyperlinks to resources in the online resources for this book. Look there first, before trying to create new resources; you may not find anything perfect but you might find a lot of the groundwork has been done for you!

Bonus idea ★

Every time you visit another school or talk to a teacher from another school, ask if they would be happy to share their favourite resource with you.

Using technology

'I've always got my phone with me – it's the best way to contact me about my child, by text or email.'

The right technology can help create a platform to boost home-school communication. Recent studies have shown that using texts to alert parents to upcoming exams, for example, can support achievement.

There is a very wide range of resources available to schools that can be used to help communicate with parents, and to support the home learning environment. We aren't recommending any particular product, but before choosing one, consider:

- Do you want to be able to message all parents all the time? Or do you need a programme that will let you set groups, such as year groups or clubs?
- Do you want a programme that sends texts or one that sends push notifications? The first lets you ensure that everyone gets the message but also requires you to have up-to-date information about phone numbers for everyone. The second appear on parents' smartphones, like notifications from social media.
- How often will you use the programme, and do you want to send pictures? (Sending photos of work or groups is a great way to keep parents involved.)

Having said all that, don't neglect old-fashioned technology. The phone can be a wonderful thing; just phoning a parent to tell them how well their child is doing, or something good they did that day, can make all the difference.

- Many smartphones can translate texts into different languages – let parents know about this with clear instructions, if it would be of use.
- Don't overload parents (just as you don't overload pupils with new information). Little and often is better – distinguish between what parents need to know far in advance (dates, times, things that might be expensive and need budgeting) and things that can be sent home 'just in time'.
- Know the difference between giving information and having a dialogue – make sure you don't do one when the other is required!
- Start a class blog to get the children involved.

And nothing will ever replace talking face-to-face!

Bonus idea ★

One school we know of live streams a 'good work' assembly so parents can see their child's work and industry being celebrated without having to physically attend.

Don't go it alone

'Some of the best CPD I ever do is at lunches at conferences –
because then I can talk to other teachers and find out what actually
works for them!'

**For all that school are busy places, they can be quite isolated –
and isolating. Schools often operate as more or less autonomous
entities; you may interact with other agencies, but how often do
you link up with other schools or other practitioners?**

There are apps for
phones that will not only
copy people's business
cards, but then add their
information to your
contacts. Make sure you
have an app like that
before your next event
with other teachers!

Research and anecdote both suggest that the
most valuable type of CPD for teachers is often
professional discussion with other teachers.
But, precisely because schools are such busy
places, it can be very difficult to find the time
or the opportunity to have those professional
discussions, in or out of school.

In school

- Set aside time during an INSET day – or,
  better still, a series of INSET days – to talk
  about ideas around parental engagement.
- Create a bank of good ideas to share.
- When new staff arrive, see if they can add to
  the bank of resources/ideas – make this a
  formal part of their induction.

Out of school

- Link up with other local schools to do some
  of the activities above, perhaps structuring
  the discussion around the framework of
  'good now, even better if' or 'new ideas to
  try'.
- Don't be shy about sharing good practice.
  You tell pupils they should celebrate their
  successes, and this applies to teachers as well.
- Arrange joint training/meetings around
  parental engagement with the secondary
  schools your pupils go to help ease transition.

Your school website

'I gave up trying to find anything on the website – there's no index and everything is out of date.'

The website is the primary advertisement for the school and needs to serve the practical purpose of signposting parents to appropriate information. It also defines the relationship with home and school.

Often the first port of call for parents exploring a new school for their child is the school website. They explore what the headteacher says about the school – its ethos, values and approach to teaching and developing children.

In an ideal world, the school website will speak of home-school partnership and celebrate the way in which the school works with families. The school will demonstrate this through several means:

- the inclusive and positive language it uses in its description of school values and ethos
- an online description or depiction of its parental engagement activities
- images that it chooses to place on the site
- flagging examples of how family partnership actually works in practice
- a section on learning for families
- a glossary of school language and terminology
- an FAQ section
- an easy-to-navigate structure
- making sure that the information on the site is kept up to date.

Sometimes, if schools don't prioritise the upkeep of a website, it can rapidly become like a neglected garden: untidy, unattractive and unused.

Teaching tip

A website with up-to-date, live information is invaluable to parents. It's easier said than done, but definitely worth the effort!

Bonus idea ★

Find out if there is a parent within the community who is IT savvy and happy to upload material to the site from time to time. It's nice to have a parent contributing to the site in this way because it means they can let you know if there's anything else that needs to go up on the site to make it more parent-friendly. Having their views on board is worth its weight in gold.

Being a reflective practitioner

'You've already enjoyed lots of positive interactions with parents in your career. Sit down for a moment and think about that.'

What we're asking for in this book requires some pretty fundamental changes to the way teachers think about their work with parents. Those changes need to be thought about carefully.

It's remarkably easy to get discouraged, particularly if you are working to change a culture that is entrenched in a school or a parent body. So, it's important – for your own wellbeing as well as for moving things forward and eliciting help from others – to acknowledge when things do go well. As a teacher, you know how important praise is for people who are learning. In this idea, 'people who are learning' includes you (and your colleagues!).

Here are some ideas to think about:

- Think of times when parent partnership has really worked for you and share with colleagues.
- Have a noticeboard in the staffroom where you share feedback from parents that was positive about homework/home learning, etc. This board should also reference the school vision and values when it comes to parent partnership.
- Someone might take responsibility for sharing tips of the week for parents here, that others can send home by way of text, for example.
- Think about the results you get from your work on supporting parental engagement in the most positive (but honest) way possible. Only five parents came to the 'Making Maths Work' workshop? OK, that's not many – but you've begun to build relationships with those five families, and that's a win.

- Remember the 'even better if' mantra – anything you've done to this point can be a building block for the future.
- Keeping records along the lines we have suggested means you will be more able to think back on what's happened lately.
- Remember to reflect on the good points as well as the ones that still need improvement.
- Treat engagement with parents the way you treat other parts of your professional practice – as something that can always be improved, about which you can always learn.
- Reflection doesn't need to be a solo activity. Try to work with others as often as possible – after all, relationships and interaction are at the basis of all good engagement.
- When a conversation with a parent goes really well, try to consider why that was the case.
- Being reflective doesn't necessarily mean about yourself and your practice. You may see a colleague interacting positively with a parent or family and consider that there is something to learn from their approach.
- If a parent asks you a question or emails you about something, don't be afraid to say that you are not quite sure of the answer or that you need to give it some thought. They will value your response so much more when you do eventually reply, because you have put thought into your reply.

Bonus idea ★

Giving feedback to colleagues is a lovely way to start or end the week. Instead of Secret Santa this year, staff could exchange professional compliments with another member of staff. They may pull out a specific example from over the year where a colleague has gone above and beyond the call of duty, or refer to a child that they feel their colleague has been instrumental in helping to make good progress. Compliments are seldom given but go a long way!

Talk to your SENCO (and PSO if you have one!)

'No one knows our families as well as our SENCO – I was amazed what I learned from her!'

Just by the nature of their jobs, some people work more closely with parents than other members of a school community. Use their knowledge!

Special educational needs coordinators, family or parental support officers, attendance officers, reception staff – these members of the school staff often work very closely with parents or interact with them more frequently than class teachers. One of the messages of this book is that supporting parental engagement need not add to teacher workload, but that requires going about it in the most efficient manner possible. It means using all of the resources and knowledge to hand as effectively as possible.

- Ensure that all members of staff have appropriate access to the records we have been talking about, so that they can add their ideas.
- There's a fine line between sharing information for the benefit of children and gossiping about families. It's important to have that line clear for everyone in the school community. Use an INSET day, or part of one, to discuss this and create some guidelines.
- Your SENCO will have had training and will have amassed skills through their work with families – ask them for their top tips.
- If you have a parent or family support officer (FSO, PSO – they go by a range of names), include them in discussions around supporting parents.

You've got this! But it's not finished yet...

'Once I realised how important parental engagement was, I realised it's not something you tick off – it's something you live.'

Just as one is never finished teaching, because there are always new children who need to learn, parental engagement is never finished – there are always new families to engage with.

- Remember to re-run the parental survey and audit (see Idea 23) at least once every two years, or every year if possible.
- When children join the school midway through the year, make sure that you find out about the families, and make contact with them as soon as you can.
- Once new parents have had a chance to settle into the school, ask them to fill in the parental survey – and remember that they may need extra invitations to things.
- Families joining a school need to adjust, just like the children do!
- Transition is your best possible opportunity to get to know families and children.
- Keeping good records will make it much easier to carry on work from year to year.
- Doing evaluation well means that you will know what to continue doing – and, importantly, what's not worth carrying on with!

Teaching tip

Remember, it's just as important to celebrate your own successes as it is to celebrate those of the children in your class. That's particularly the case if you're starting from scratch in this area!